ENLIGHTENED
MANAGEMENT

Insights on Creating a Respectful,
Dignified, and Successful Work Environment

ALEJANDRO DIAZ

Ordering Information: To order in bulk, contact the author at the e-mail address above.

For more information about the author, visit www.dandems.com.

Text by Alejandro Diaz
Book cover and design by Kris Avilla, www.artlabkma.com
Copy edited by Nicole Frail, www.nicolefrail.com

Also available as an ebook.

Printed in the United States of America

First edition, printed November 2023

DEDICATION

This book is dedicated to my parents, who showed me that faith, courage, honesty, kindness, and hard work could make dreams a reality.

CONTENTS

INTRODUCTION

I have worked at many places throughout the thirty-five years of my professional career. Like most people, I have had ups and downs with my bosses. I have experienced the good manager, the bad manager, and the very ugly manager, leading me to the conclusion that there are basically two types of managers: enlightened and unenlightened.

An Enlightened Manager is a visionary, a leader; open, flexible, and honest, he or she is someone who brings humanity to the office every day. An Unenlightened manager is the complete opposite. This person is shortsighted, often dishonest, and at times even cruel. Unenlightened managers can create a dysfunctional, disrespectful, and downright mean-spirited work setting.

Through this book, I will show how being an Enlightened Manager is the best way to bring fulfillment to the greatest number of people in our places of business. My intention is not to write a management manual but rather to show how respect, dignity, empathy, and humanity will always make for a better work world.

My goal is to offer a unique management philosophy based on humanity first and foremost, one that will have a positive influence on our society as a whole.

I would like to pose one very important question to you before we continue: If one of your employees suddenly passed away, would that person's family welcome you to the funeral as someone who'd had a positive impact on their loved one's life? Or would you be unwelcome in their moment of grief for having made their loved one miserable Monday through Friday, 9 a.m. to 5 p.m.? This is something to really think about every morning as you start your day. Treat your staff with respect and dignity. If you do, you will always have a clear conscience, and when it's all said and done, people will remember you fondly.

One afternoon, I struck up a conversation with a woman at a store. She looked a bit sad. It turned out she was looking for a sympathy card. She told me that someone she had worked for, many years back, had passed away. This person had been her boss and was very kind and considerate to her and she always remembered that. Now, many years later, she was mourning his passing. I was moved by her genuine sadness, especially after all the time that had gone by. I also felt proud of this manager for treating her, his employee, with humanity and for leaving such a positive, long-lasting impression on a fellow human being.

Kindness should be practiced always, at home and at work. It amazes me how some people are perfectly fine human beings in their social lives, but once in the work world, they morph into ogres. There should not be a distinction between how you treat people outside of work and how you treat them at your place of business. There are no boundaries when it comes to behaving like a decent person.

We spend on average eight to ten hours a day at work, five days a week, and we all want to feel good about our jobs and about the relationships we have with those we spend so much time with. Being a manager is a huge responsibility that should never be taken lightly. You have the power to make your staff love, hate, or be ambivalent about their jobs. You can make them look forward to coming into the office or you can make them dread it. You can empower them, or you can undermine them. You can make them feel part of a team or make them feel isolated. You can also make them feel unfulfilled, depressed, unappreciated, or downright angry. Or you can make your staff feel happy, motivated, and loyal. An Enlightened Manager will have a positive effect on all his or her employees.

In today's innovative and competitive world, we have options. Workers are looking for, yes, a place that offers a good salary and benefits, but more importantly, they're looking for a place where they feel valued, respected, and empowered, a place where they can contribute and be fulfilled.

> **79% of Americans would take a pay cut to work for a more "just" company.**
> —*Washington Post*, November 9, 2017

Our offices are unique places. We are thrown in with people with whom, under ordinary circumstances, we would have never chosen to spend so much time. They are places where memories, good and bad, will be formed. They are places where people connect and sometimes become lifelong friends. They are places where daily life is shared with coworkers—marriages, divorces, engagements, illnesses, and deaths. The connections people make at the office can be life altering. We are all human beings; as social creatures, we long to form meaningful bonds with others, and our jobs are a perfect setting for this.

After spending many years in the workforce and speaking to hundreds of people about their jobs, I have learned that the workplace can also be filled with landmines, which cause enormous stress, depression, and angst. Sadly, most people I have spoken to about their jobs felt unhappy and dissatisfied in their places of employment.

The cause of this distress is almost always connected to the people in charge: the bosses.

Why is this? Are most people just inclined to dislike their bosses? Or do we have a system that doesn't place enough importance on good, solid interpersonal skills, instead promoting an environment driven only by supposed "results," where frontline employees are not valued and where shortsighted managers are seen as successful simply because they are constantly distressing their staff about every little thing?

In my opinion, it is the latter. Taking a closer look at these "hands-on" managers will show that they are hindering growth, stifling innovation, and producing limited results instead of boundless possibilities. Fulfilled employees will always show better results than scared, intimidated, task-driven workers.

I've experienced managers being disrespectful, condescending, underhanded, untrustworthy, and sometimes downright nasty. This type of behavior is not only reprehensible, but it is also unproductive, a complete waste of time and money, and totally unnecessary. People will never meet their full potential under these conditions, so this management style does indeed affect the bottom line negatively.

Fact: 57 percent of people leave their jobs because of their bosses.
—The Frontline Leader Project:
Exploring the Most Critical Segment of Leaders

I run into people all the time who have given their careers/lives to their companies but still feel unappreciated and disrespected by their bosses. These are folks who are smart, hardworking, reliable, and loyal, who have always given 100 percent to their jobs. I've often wondered why our places of work are so negative, dysfunctional, and unfulfilling for so many people. Is it that those who rise to positions of authority are geared toward dysfunction? Are the wrong people being promoted to these positions? Or is it that there's no will from the top to make things better for everyone? I have concluded that it is a mixture of all the above.

"Horrible bosses" are much too common. I have known people who have stayed in their jobs much longer than they could have ever imagined, even though they would like to make more money or take on more responsibilities, simply because they felt extremely lucky to have a decent boss. They are so fearful of starting a new job and possibly working for a monster (they've heard the horror stories or have previously had bad experiences themselves) that they keep their ambitions in check. It's as if they're frozen by fear.

How is this allowed? Management needs to be held accountable, especially when they abuse their power over staff. This behavior is not morally right and can be very costly to an organization in many ways, including low morale, low productivity, high turnover rates, frequent stress leaves, potential lawsuits, and arbitration.

At most places I've worked, the staff was in desperate need of a positive, respectful, successful, and gratifying environment. Many of them didn't know how to voice this but were all in agreement that there must be a better way. My main goal at every job I've held has been to make that place more efficient, more productive, and just as important, to make people feel good about coming to work every day. I have made sure to provide as much of this respectful and successful environment as I could. I have managed staff and coordinated office operations with diligence, efficiency, great interpersonal skills, and dignity. Unfortunately, as a midlevel manager, I often did not have the final say; I had to work under the constraints of my positions. I often reported to people who didn't share this way of looking at the work world. They were dogmatic in their dealings with their staff; to them, people were just tools that could be used to move ahead and to make their superiors happy. There is nothing wrong with personal ambition, but you don't have to mistreat people to meet your professional goals.

I saw this behavior repeatedly—some exhibited it worse than others—but there weren't enough leaders with the vision of making the office a great environment for all to thrive in as part of an organization's mission to succeed. There was never a sense of urgency to combat bad management; it was accepted as part of the status quo. This is a crucial mistake on an organization's part. Staff satisfaction should always be a priority; at the end of the day, it is important for the bottom line. Every office worker I've come across wants nothing less than to earn their paycheck week after week and to feel good about their jobs. Unfortunately, unskilled managers always seem to get in the way of attaining this feeling of complete job satisfaction.

> **Bad managers cost the US economy $550 billion each year, due to their negative impact on employee engagement.**
> —"The 10 Reasons People Really Quit Their Jobs"
> by RecruitLoop, October 28, 2015

What most people long for in the workplace is respect, appreciation, an opportunity to contribute meaningfully, and the ability to work with dignity. I don't feel that this is unreasonable or unattainable. In fact, I think it is something that should be the rule in every business, not the exception. This is why I felt the need to write *Enlightened Management*—to help us all understand that there's a better way.

This book will give you a different perspective on longstanding notions of managing. Through my professional and life experiences, I give real examples of how to manage with respect, empathy, trust, transparency, introspection, and with true leadership, which will lead to success and positive outcomes for all.

No matter what industry—tech, startups, finance, healthcare, service, academia, construction—the way management treat their staff will have an ongoing effect on the economic strength and stability of any organization. As long as human beings are still performing most jobs, it is imperative to treat everyone with respect and dignity in the workplace. If this is achieved, an organization's/company's potential will be limitless.

CHAPTER 1: WHO I AM

I was born and raised on the Southside of Chicago. My parents were Mexican immigrants who were respectful, dignified, hardworking, and trustworthy people. They instilled these traits in me and in my siblings. My upbringing and growing up in working class Chicago shaped how I came to see the world.

My father worked ten- to twelve-hour days at a paint factory, and my mother worked nights cleaning offices in Downtown Chicago. No matter how cold it was, or how much snow there was on the ground, neither of them ever missed a day of work. They didn't work hard to become rich; they worked hard to provide their family a home and a good education. My siblings and I have an amazing work ethic because of the example our parents gave us.

I got my very first job when I was a sophomore in high school. My sister recommended me for a position at a plumbing supply company where she was the office manager. I worked sixteen hours a week; eight hours sprinkled between Monday and Friday and a full eight-hour shift on Saturday. I did everything from stocking supplies, making deliveries, and cleaning the bathrooms to washing the owner's Cadillac. My sister made sure I was at work on time and that I busted my butt. It was her reputation at stake, and she wanted to be sure I made her proud.

The owner was a gruff but fair man who liked me. One day, he called me to his office and told me how much he appreciated my work but said that he wanted to make sure I had higher aspirations. He told me that I was a smart kid and that I should go to college so I wouldn't have to work menial jobs like this the rest of my life. I deeply appreciated his advice and saw firsthand how mentoring plays a big role in boss–worker relationships. Taking a real interest in your employees' careers and well-being is essential for developing a solid relationship with your staff.

After high school, I got a job with UPS. Here, I honed my skills as a manager. I started out unloading packages from trailers; it was a physically demanding job, but I mastered it. I was one of the fastest "unloaders" in the hub, and as a result, I then became a package sorter, which paid more. I mastered that and was soon promoted to a supervisory position.

As a supervisor, I spent a lot of time training and developing my staff, and they became the best team there. UPS taught me how to train, train, cross-train, and retrain employees. They made it clear that they made a big investment in every employee; they hated losing workers because it cost money to hire and train them and it cost even more money to hire and train their replacements. That's exactly how they put it, and this has stuck with me ever since.

I believe that terminating subordinates for a lack of productivity should be an absolute last resort. For the most part, I feel that you can turn mediocre employees into great ones by simply working with them. Put in the time to properly train your employees. It will pay off.

While working at UPS, I started attending college, but I must admit that I wasn't too interested. I really enjoyed my job at UPS, and I was hoping to make a career out of it. So, I dropped out of the university after only one semester.

My father had always emphasized the importance of getting a college education. Even though he didn't have one himself, he knew that a university degree meant much more than just a ticket to climb the corporate ladder. He knew that it was about knowledge and exposure to different ways of thinking. It indeed broadens one's horizons, as they say. My father wanted his children to be educated people. He would always say that once we earned our degrees, no one could ever take them away from us. My younger brother took our father's advice from the outset, and right after high school went off to college to get that degree that my father advocated so vehemently for.

After a few years away from school, and much cajoling from my little brother, I finally went back to college and earned my bachelor of arts from the University of Illinois at Chicago (UIC). I loved my political science and Latin-American Studies classes and the other courses that encouraged critical thinking. I was not drawn to stringent, concentrated fields like accounting or engineering. I thrived on the well-rounded curriculum that a liberal arts degree offered. It showed me that the world was very diverse and that there were different ways of looking at things. This proved essential to how I approached life from then on.

After college, I continued working at UPS but soon realized that I wanted to further pursue the arts. I quit my job of eleven years, went off to film school, and earned a master of fine arts in screenwriting from the University of Miami. I then moved out to Los Angeles to try telling my stories through film. After several years trying to "make it" in the film industry, I realized that that wasn't for me after all. I went back into the corporate world and saw that I could use my creative talents to promote a unique work environment, one based on respect, dignity, and innovation. I've seen how creativity and great interpersonal skills can foster a win-win situation for all, management and regular staff alike. But it takes effort, willingness, and the right attitude to accomplish this.

THE OLD MAN IN ACTION

While at UPS, another young supervisor who shared a similar working-class background with me admired my success. I was productive, fair, and well-liked by my crew. His name was Elmer, and he too was hardworking, but he noticed a difference between us. For him, leading people was difficult, and he felt it came much more naturally to me. One day, while sitting in the break room, Elmer asked me what my father did for a living. Many of us were first-generation Americans with mothers and fathers who worked blue-collar jobs. I told him that my father was a manager at a paint factory. Elmer sat back to think for a bit, then said, "There's where you get it from." He went on to tell me that his father was a factory worker, and that supervising people was quite alien to him. At the time, I didn't think too much about Elmer's comments, but a few years later, I realized that he'd had a point.

My father came to this country penniless. He dreamed of giving his family the life he was never able to acquire in his own country. He was young, smart, strong, and had a great work ethic. When he first arrived here, he worked many menial jobs: farm laborer in the Florida orange groves, bartender, plant assembly line, etc.

Then he got a very good job at a paint factory as a production manager in 1972. He was highly recommended by his younger brother, my Uncle Ernesto (Tio Neto). Tio Neto was just as charismatic as my father but was restless. Tio Neto had been the production manager at this company for a few years but decided that he wanted to move back to Mexico. When he gave his resignation to the owners of the plant, he told them that he had the perfect replacement—his brother, my father. The owners of the company, Mel and Shel, loved my Tio Neto and were very sorry to see him go. But he told them not to worry, that his brother "was just like him." Mel and Shel respected my uncle so much that they hired my father unseen, no résumé, and without an interview, on the spot. Papi started that very next Monday morning.

This job would finally allow my father to provide for his family in the way he had always dreamed. He worked six days a week, and on Saturdays he'd take me and my younger brother to see him in action. My father was a tall, gregarious man who was charming, but if he needed to be firm, he would do so without hesitation.

On those Saturday mornings, my brother and I would walk the floor with him. It seemed as if he knew everyone and that everyone loved him, from the workers to the other managers to the actual owners of the plant. My father would check up on all his employees, making sure they were doing their jobs correctly and in a timely manner, and providing them with the resources needed to complete their tasks. It was magical to see him in action. He spoke English with an accent but was nonetheless a fantastic communicator. He was able to give clear directions to workers and at the same time give precise and timely updates to his bosses, the factory owners. In short, my father was smart and tough but fair and enthusiastic. His staff worked hard for him and were very loyal. Papi always treated his employees with the utmost respect; he was hardworking and committed to the overall success of the company. My father was a true leader. So yes, my friend Elmer was definitely onto something. I did indeed learn many great lessons watching my old man run that paint factory those many years back in Chicago.

Aside from having a great work ethic, my parents were also very principled. They taught us to always treat people how we'd like to be treated—with respect and dignity—and to have empathy for our fellow human beings. A strong work ethic along with being ethical, honest, and sincere are must-haves to be a real leader.

UPS Years

The UPS hub I worked at was on the East Side of Chicago. Back in those days, it was a very tough area, and many UPS employees were from some of the roughest parts of the city. Most of us were from

5

working-class neighborhoods; we were paying our own way through school or looking for stable careers. UPS not only taught me some very valuable management skills, but it also helped me pay for my college education.

It was a very fast-paced environment full of testosterone, a very physically intensive job. In my work area, there were rows and rows of bays with trucks in each one of them. The trailers were filled with hundreds, sometimes thousands, of packages. On one side of the plant floor were the trailers and unloaders, on the other side, with fast-moving belts in between, were the package sorters.

The unloaders had to empty the trailers as quickly as possible while following all the safety requirements. When I'd look across the rows of belts, ideally I'd see the packages come out of the trailers back-to-back, no space between them, with all the labels facing up on the fast-moving conveyors. The packages would stream across to the other side where the package sorters were waiting to sort them. On the sorter side, there were several belts, or slides, with various colors, some were on the floor, some were waist high, and some were at shoulder height.

The supervisors trained the unloaders to unload their trailers properly and efficiently. We taught them to cautiously open the truck doors, so as not to be crushed by the hundreds of packages that lay behind. We trained them to get close to the packages, to grab the boxes with both hands, to keep their backs straight, and to lift with their legs. They were provided stepstools to reach the top of the trailers and small baskets in which they'd place envelopes. We also taught them how to place every parcel on the conveyor belt with its label facing up so the sorter on the other end would be able to read the label quickly and then place it on the appropriate colored belt. We showed them how to unload a trailer as safely and as quickly as humanly possible.

The parcel sorters were paid a dollar more an hour than the unloaders; they had to pass a test showing that they knew what color belt every single US zip code went to. Each belt represented states and/or zip codes. For example, Ohio was the black belt, Illinois went to the yellow belt, Florida was the gold belt.

The package sorters had to keep up with the unloader's pace, because if they fell behind, the scene could quickly turn chaotic. It was the supervisor's job to make sure things ran smoothly. Once properly sorted, the packages would ride the pulley system (which was made up of miles and miles of steel and rubber that ran throughout the huge facility), finally reaching empty waiting trailers where loaders would load them up to reach their final destinations. The whole system was genius, an engineering feat.

As a supervisor, I trained and retrained my sorters and unloaders to be the very best. The teams were made up mostly of young men and women who could perform this labor-intensive job. I would make it into a game; it was always a friendly competition, seeing who would do the best job that night. I would walk up and down the aisles pumping them up. If I saw that there were issues, I'd jump right in and either help my staff catch up or retrain them on best practices. They reacted very positively to my gusto. Enthusiasm is contagious! I shined because I made it fun every evening and my crew liked as well as respected me.

Being positive, helpful, and enthusiastic with your people will always motivate them to reach higher.

UPS taught me how to be productive. The company invested a lot of money in time studies. They knew how much output an employee should produce within a given time frame to be successful. Their expectations were high but never unreasonable. It is good to have a high bar, but you must give your staff the proper training and tools to reach it. Your goals must also be attainable or else you will frustrate your staff and squash their enthusiasm.

I had also developed a great relationship with the command center; I was always on top of my work, and they knew that we could handle the tougher loads if they were in a bind. We had to finish all our work within a five-hour timeframe, making sure that everything was spotless and ready to go for the next shift. Every night, we were up for and met the challenge. Throughout my career, I have always tried to bring out the very best in all the people I work with. That is what a great manager focuses on. How to get something done without being a complete jerk about it? It all starts with a strong foundation of respect and trust.

One employee of mine at UPS was a tough young man from a rough part of town. All the other supervisors who worked with him thought he was merely a lazy troublemaker and avoided him at all costs. But I knew he had great potential, because I had seen firsthand how much talent he had when he put his mind to it.

When he worked for me, he was fantastic. What made our relationship different was something very simple. After working with him a couple times, I quickly learned that he liked going home early. So, I made a deal with him: if he would bust his butt for me, he'd be the first one out. Lo and behold, every time he came to my area, he'd work like a madman, and I'd always let him be the first one to clock out. Of course, I first made sure the rest of my team was okay with this, and they were. They wanted more hours, he didn't.

When one of the other managers asked him why he worked so hard for me, he simply said that I was tough but that I always treated him fairly. When I heard this feedback, it made me proud. This great employee did not respond to threats or any other form of intimidation; he responded to fairness. Leaders must be flexible and deal with their employees as individuals. Tailor your management style to each team member. You'd be surprised what motivates people. Some may want to be showered with praise, others may just ask for a simple thank-you, and some may want new and challenging projects. There is no one single motivator. It's your job to find the right mix.

As a manager, you must invest the time in getting to know each team member individually. If you have an employee who doesn't seem to be giving their all, find out what motivates this person, then work at motivating them. A little change in outlook can go a long way.

It is also important to be a person of your word. Don't go back on your promises—see them through. If I had not kept my promise to that young man at UPS and did not let him go home after busting his butt, then he wouldn't have worked hard for me ever again. Trust is the foundation for any strong relationship.

KEEPING THINGS IN CONTEXT

One day, my UPS manager brought over a new employee to join my unloading team. He was an older (compared to my crew of college-aged people) Polish American man named John. He had worked for the company for more than thirty years as a driver. His eyesight was now poor, so they had to find another position for him before he retired. They gave him to me. I was in my twenties, and he was closer to my father's age, so intuitively, I was very respectful toward him. He was a nice guy who came in every day ready to work.

As was my norm, I trained my new team member on the proper and quickest way to unload a trailer. John worked hard and followed the proper process to a tee, but he was nowhere near as fast as my slowest unloader. My manager noticed this and started riding me for John's slow output. I kept working with John, but unloading was a younger person's job. My manager didn't let up, telling me that I needed to put more pressure on my new employee to up his game. I refused.

I told my boss that I wasn't going to be responsible for John having a heart attack. The way I looked at it, John had put in many years of good service, and had always been an exemplary employee, so I wasn't about to give him a hard time just because I could. My boss then relented. I was later notified that John had been moved to the custodial department, where the physical aspect of the job was much more forgiving. He could now work his last couple of years with dignity.

One afternoon, after John had transferred, I ran into him, and we chatted a bit. John told me that he knew I had been under a lot of pressure because of his low productivity and that he'd felt bad about this. He apologized for it. I told him that there was no need to be sorry, that I knew he had been trying his very best. John then shook my hand and thanked me for always treating him with respect. This was a proud moment for me. John was someone's father, somone's husband, someone's son, someone's uncle. Wouldn't you want your family member always treated with the utmost respect?

I will always be grateful for all that I learned and experienced at UPS. I learned how to motivate teams, how to train and retrain employees, how to tailor my management style to the individual, how to succeed. I have used, and continue to use, many of those lessons from that time to this very day.

CHAPTER 2: HIRING, TRAINING & MANAGING MANAGERS

WE NEED REAL LEADERS

As I noted earlier, managing people is a huge responsibility. So, it is crucial to promote/hire the right folks. Too many times, people are put in leadership positions who aren't leaders. Big mistake.

Individuals who shine in one specific area are usually rewarded with managerial promotions. It doesn't matter whether these people ever had any experience supervising staff; they are still promoted to lead teams and, at times, entire departments. They may be hardworking, diligent employees—even experts in their fields—but these things alone don't make them leaders. You may feel compelled to reward them by promoting them to leadership positions, but they may not necessarily be the ones who will lead your staff, your organization, to reaching its full potential.

We need real leaders! Real leaders speak up when something is not right. They don't ignore obvious misconduct. They are fair, they treat everyone equally, and they don't show favoritism. When you allow some employees to enjoy some fringe benefits, like leaving early or working remote, and don't give these same opportunities to all, it breeds resentment, mistrust, and low morale.

In order to manage staff, if possible, the person being considered for a management post should, ideally, have a couple of years of experience under their belt leading teams in one capacity or another. Or at the very least, they should be able to show leadership qualities through solid examples from their careers or their academic years.

Have them also give you at least two references from people they've actually managed. If they haven't technically managed staff, they can give you the names of colleagues whom they've worked closely on specific projects. Call these references and find out about their experiences reporting to this candidate. This should be a vital part of your final decision.

You can hold all the team building and professional training events in the world, but if your managers are not decent people, this will just be a huge waste of time and money. To optimize your workforce, you need managers who have great interpersonal skills, are respectful, and can motivate your staff daily. I have experienced and heard of bad managers taking advantage of their authority to intimidate and harass their staff. This happens much too often, and it always infuriates me when this occurs. People who behave this way should not be in leadership positions; they shouldn't manage one single person.

There should be, at the least, a few months of training and ongoing evaluation of how that person manages their staff. Frontline employees need to be involved in this training period and should be asked for honest feedback for this process to really work. Staff should be assured that their comments and suggestions will not be taken negatively, nor will there be any retaliation. I know many organizations will be reluctant to do this because of the longstanding authoritarian tradition that exists in many of our workplaces. Yes, there must be people in charge who have the authority to make crucial decisions, but we should strive to form partnerships with staff, and move away from the old-school "I'm the boss, do it my way or take the highway" mentality.

True leaders are visionaries. They have courage, they have empathy, and they are creative and kind. Real leaders don't get bogged down and stuck on minute details; they are always focused on the bigger picture, the end game. I have seen firsthand many great employees stunted by managers who were shortsighted.

These supervisors were always caught up, almost obsessively, with minor details that in the long run were insignificant. Unfortunately, many wonderful employees are driven out and never truly appreciated for their worth, never allowed to flourish in their roles under this type of boss. It is vital to identify principled people and train them for managerial positions. In too many instances, organizations don't spend enough time and effort ensuring their managers are real leaders who will lead their teams to ultimate success.

Promoting, hiring, or training a new manager is something that should be taken very seriously. Again, I have seen people who are very good at their specific jobs be rewarded through a promotion to a management position, but one thing really has nothing to do with the other. I've had experience with great employees who make mediocre and even horrible managers. You will be way ahead of the game if you simply hire the right management team to begin with.

> **Jim Clifton, Chairman and CEO of Gallup, once wrote, "The single biggest decision you make in your job—bigger than all the rest—is who you name manager. When you name the wrong person manager, nothing fixes that bad decision. Not compensation, not benefits—nothing."**

A smart organization will take promoting or hiring a new manager seriously. I am not simply talking about signing up new managers for those cookie-cutter, run-of-the-mill trainings. What I mean is showing new managers how to behave professionally and respectfully with staff.

You would be surprised how many managers do not have the basic interpersonal skills needed to effectively manage. These include simple things like being honest, being fair, showing respect, being sincere—these are somehow quite foreign to some people. If you can't behave like a decent human being every day, you shouldn't manage people, period.

MANAGING MANAGERS

In my opinion, executives are often too close to their frontline directors, and at times refuse to see the dysfunction that may lie below. This is not only unfortunate but also a huge mistake. Upper management are supposed to be leaders for all and not just best friends with their direct reports. They must be objective and continually keep their fingers on the pulse of all their employees. It is a fact that employees who feel valued, trust their bosses, enjoy the camaraderie in the office, and are satisfied with their workload are much more productive and effective. These departments shine.

On the other hand, in departments where the employees often feel intimidated, unappreciated, undermined, and not supported, those employees will never fulfill their potential. These latter departments will spend so much time trying to find their way around the dysfunction that they will never find their rhythm and will just keep spinning in a never-ending destructive cycle. The head of a department has authority and will influence their work environment to be positive or negative. Which would you prefer?

POINTERS FOR MANAGERS WHO MANAGE MANAGERS:

- Take the time to train them.
- Observe them in their daily interactions with their teams.
- Get consistent feedback from frontline staff.

- Be available to all your people; assure them that you're in their corner, too.
- Don't show favoritism toward your management team/ special club.
- Have sincere conversations with your managers about issues brought to your attention. "Feed back and forth"—feedback should be a two-way street.
- Immediately address and stop unethical behaviors by your managers.
- Mentor them on how to always behave with professional respect.
- Don't ignore red flags!
- Have staff evaluate managers routinely and look at results seriously.
- You are responsible for all employees in your department, so be a leader to all of them.

EVALUATING MANAGERS

STAFF RETENTION!

Retaining and keeping talent should be a priority in any organization. The best way to minimize your turnover rate is by showing your staff that you value them. Some employees like public acknowledgment, some want to be challenged with higher levels of responsibility, some want raises, others enjoy taking time off, and for some, a simple thank-you will go a long way. Survey your staff to find their preferences. Individualize how you show appreciation to each one of your team members and do it often. Talented employees will look for other opportunities if they're not happy. Value their contributions and don't ever take them for granted. Once you start losing valuable team members, it can turn into a domino effect; before you know it, most of your team is gone, leading to work overload for the remaining staff, missed deadlines, and a declining quality of work. Overworked employees will soon start looking for more balanced jobs.

> **"In respectful workplaces, employees are more engaged and productive. In workplaces with little or no respect, employees report more conflicts and misunderstandings and lower attendance and productivity."**
>
> —"6 Transformative Benefits of Respect in the Workplace" by Johnny Duncan

When people feel valued, they're empowered. When staff feel empowered, they are vested and enthusiastic; they look forward to going to work to take on the next challenge. When people feel mistreated and undervalued, they will not give their best and will never reach their full potential. They will dream of a better place and will leave for greener pastures as soon as the opportunity arises. An Enlightened Manager will be creative and put in the time to keep their staff happy and productive.

Staff retention and job satisfaction should be a marker followed very closely when evaluating managers. Company leaders should have their staff evaluate their managers quarterly, or at the very least, to coincide with the traditional evaluation timeline. In most organizations, evaluations are a one-way street: managers evaluating their employees. Well, there are two sides to every story, so staff should evaluate managers periodically, as well.

If a department is in total chaos and good people come and go, this will cost an organization dearly. It's astonishing how many companies allow their upper management personnel to continue with dysfunctional practices unabated. It's time to stop this madness. The first sign of bad managerial habits should automatically be looked into, monitored, and corrected. All institutions, big and small, need to take their staff's job satisfaction indices much more seriously. Management should be evaluated frequently on how their staff feels working for them.

A very simple survey, with the right questions, will give an indication of what is really happening in your workplace. The leadership of any organization should look closely at a manager's turnover rate. If it's high, there's probably some underlying dysfunction in the environment. Action should be taken much sooner than later. Don't ever lose good staff because of an unenlightened manager!

ACCOUNTABILITY FOR ALL: HOLDING BAD MANAGERS ACCOUNTABLE

I once worked for a director who oversaw an entire department. This person had never even managed one staff member prior to getting this important position. This person had been promoted without the experience, education, or all-around know-how. This administrator's mantra, as shared with staff, was "fake it 'til you make it." A good manager doesn't fake it. No one has all the answers; if you don't know something, admit it and be willing to learn. Don't be arrogant about your ignorance.

This inexperienced manager had a clear agenda: to get to the top of the heap at any cost. This person looked at employees as friends or foes. Bad managers sacrifice their employees for the sake of their own careers. They don't show humility or humanity.

To the top brass, this director was ambitious, smart, and hardworking. To those who worked for this person, they were a complete nightmare. This administrator kissed up and punched down.

Many well-established staff left the department because of this person's unethical, unprofessional behavior. There were many serious HR complaints and investigations, but nothing affected the support this person got from the organization's executives. This manager had the ears of those in positions of authority, and they never took the time to really listen to the everyday staff that were being put through the wringer on a daily basis.

It is very damaging for an organization when they allow their upper management to behave unethically with impunity. There will always be red flags to dysfunction. If there are several staff members, in good standing, who have suddenly left a division after a change in management, there is something terribly wrong. If there are numerous complaints from staff, there's something terribly wrong. If there are several HR investigations, there's something terribly wrong. Smart organizations will not allow this diseased environment to linger too long; they will nip it in the bud sooner rather than later.

In this case, the department had a high turnover rate (close to 30 percent), and staff often went on stress leaves. This organization's executives were too unenlightened to see how much they were really losing by condoning this one person's bad behavior. This all occurred at a very well-respected healthcare entity. The organization always expressed concern for the health of their customer/patient base, but they didn't seem at all concerned about the well-being of their very own employees.

I have seen it too many times; management is given carte blanche and their unscrupulous treatment of their staff is ignored. This is a bad scenario for all involved.

CONSEQUENCES

Because of the inappropriate behavior by this department's director, staff were not working up to their potential, and they were always looking over their shoulders and searching for opportunities to get out, instead of working at their optimal abilities and making the place flourish. Low productivity loses revenue; lost potential is just as costly, if not more. Instead of focusing on the work that lies ahead, staff became paranoid and were constantly preparing for the next fight. No trust, no good work.

A bad manager can cause great damage in a very short period—the loss of solid, long-standing employees, establishing a dysfunctional work environment, low morale, dwindling productivity. These are all very serious consequences that come at a deep cost to any business. I have said it before and will continue to say it: all companies must make sure that they hire the right people for their management positions, vigilantly evaluate and hold them accountable, and provide coaching or mentoring as needed.

Another director in this same organization I came across treated staff like dirt. This person was abrasive, crude, disrespectful, and even racist. But this administrator put in ten- to twelve-hour workdays and had built a brand of competence that won over the governing board. Someone I worked with put it this way: "You don't make your workhorse running back the quarterback." Just because someone works ten- to twelve-hour days doesn't make them good manager material. Managing is all about quality not quantity.

There was an exhaustive investigation concerning abuses and racist comments that this director had made. Despite this, the leaders at this facility gave this person a pass. They were sending a clear message to their employees that they did not care how this person treated them, or behaved, that all that mattered was this administrator's supposed "high performance."

The workers in the department were stunned by this inaction and by the overall handling of the situation. Morale was very low, and there was absolutely no trust in upper management after this.

To this day, I do not understand how the executives at this organization allowed this deplorable behavior to continue. It's sad to note that the higher-ups and HR did not show any concern whatsoever about this appalling situation. They just kept feeding this vicious monster, creating an overall culture of dysfunction and impunity. This was not the way to develop and promote respect; it was the complete opposite.

Every single person on your team should be valued, treated fairly, and respected. And everyone should be held accountable for his or her bad behavior. No exceptions.

"When a manager respects his or her employees, there is no room for harassment, favoritism, or bullying."

—"6 Transformative Benefits of Respect in the Workplace" by Johnny Duncan

SHARED GOVERNANCE

Autocratic managers can cause significant damage in a very short period. Where there is smoke, there is fire; if not put out immediately, it will spread quickly, causing a lot of damage, chaos, and casualties. Do not sacrifice one decent employee to unscrupulous behavior. Monitor your managers closely!

In academia, faculty is usually not unionized, but they do have an independent body often called the Academic Senate, which monitors situations that may come up that affect faculty members' well-being.

They work with the notion of Shared Governance, which basically means that we're all in this together, so we need to figure this thing out as a team. This alliance is made up of faculty members who investigate issues that are brought to them, which they then report back to the university's administration.

The Academic Senate hears complaints of abuses and improprieties, but most importantly, they make sure that their colleagues are being treated respectfully by the university administration. After reporting their concerns, they work closely with the university heads to adequately address the matters raised.

Universities take the Academic Senate's role very seriously; they know that a gratified and empowered faculty will lead to a thriving student body and optimal enrollment. This is exactly what is also needed in the corporate world. There is nothing more demoralizing than feeling disrespected and unheard. There should be a governing, non-HR body (for the most part, HR is there to "protect" an organization from legal liability, but they are not problem-solvers) made up of a variety of staff from across the organization, whose main objective is to address issues of harassment, intimidation, unfairness, and bullying. Then their findings will be formally addressed at the HR level.

This objective collective (grievance committee) will act as the thin blue line, making sure unprincipled managers do not exploit their authority by abusing or harassing their workforce. A full-time ombudsperson could also work in this role in place of a committee.

This will go a long way in protecting hardworking, dedicated, long-time staff from a fly-by-night unscrupulous boss. **Shared Governance!**

CHAPTER 3: ATTRIBUTES OF AN ENLIGHTENED MANAGER

Enlightened Managers understand that a fulfilled workforce leads to great results.

An Enlightened Manager communicates effectively, makes work interesting, is positive, challenging in a good way, gives praise when it is due, is supportive, gives constructive critiques when necessary, is honest, and is fair. You should respect your staff, share a common goal, care about them, and be flexible. This is something that not all people are qualified to do. Even if someone is quite knowledgeable, efficient, and hardworking in their specific field, this alone will not make for a good manager. It takes character, vision, charisma, empathy, courage, and experience to become an Enlightened Manager, to manage with humility and humanity.

Take a true interest in your staff's well-being. You don't have to be best friends with each of them but do behave like a human being with all of them. Always be empathetic to others. As a manager, you can control your staff's time at work. Put yourself in their shoes; make it positive. The way you treat people daily will have consequences, good or bad. Treating your team respectfully will bring that respect right back to you; treat them badly and that, too, will also come back at you. We spend a lot of time Monday through Friday at work, so why not make it a good daily experience for all? Happy employees can do amazing things. The "I'm the boss" and "you're lucky to have a job" way of managing is dysfunctional and unproductive.

Unfortunately, this old way of doing things just won't go away. It is up to you, to us, to make changes and lead our staff to the glory we all deserve.

Be confident in your humanity. Honorable managers always come from a good place. If you know that deep down in your heart you have the best of intentions for your staff, then you should go about your daily interactions with them with complete confidence.

As I made my way up the corporate rungs, I saw how working hard is by no means the only factor that decides your fate. Many times, it is not the most qualified or "best" employee who gets the promotion or the accolades. The person who may move up is the one who maneuvers around the office, makes friends with the right people, keeps their cards close to their chest, and who will do almost anything to keep that ladder strong and sturdy for the climb ahead. There is nothing wrong with personal ambition, but you don't have to leave a battlefield filled with bloodied victims in your wake. An Enlightened Manager has character, is courageous, and will always be forthright, even when it may not be the thing that will lead to an instant return. But it's the right thing to do. Enlightened Managers lead by example, always holding themselves to the highest standards.

On the next page you'll find an Enlightened Manager's perspective, from a colleague I deeply respect. This senior director has successfully led teams for many years at one of the premiere healthcare organizations in the country. This is straight from her daily playbook, in her very own words:

I lead by sticking to the basics. My approach isn't sexy or overly orchestrated, but it's effective.

The term *basics* by no means indicates simplicity or lack of importance. This basic thought process gives me a solid path for a well-rounded engagement. It's like any other relationship; it requires ongoing maintenance. The manager–staff bond only thrives with the right amount of care and attention. A thoughtful approach carries the expectation of flexibility according to the person's personality and emotional intelligence.

I use the five Ps as my pillars: personal, professional, potential, preference, and principles.

Personal: Getting to know someone, especially a staff member or colleague, on a personal level doesn't mean you must know and understand intimate information about them and their lifestyle. Rather, it refers to knowing the individual beyond their role—learning all that is important to them when they're in the workplace. Often, this may result in acquiring special nuggets that relate to their life outside of the organization. That's a bonus, especially when you become aware of events or experiences that make them happy or are currently challenging them. Knowing a staff member in a personal way equates to observing how they react in various circumstances, knowing their communication style preference (email, face to face, phone), understanding their experience (including points of reference and past roles), and caring about their priorities in and out of the office. Every quarter, I treat small groups of six to eight (non-managers) of my team from various functions to an offsite lunch, usually at a restaurant within walking distance of the office. Many of the team members do not work with me directly, so our opportunity to engage is limited and our ability to know one another beyond the hallways is even smaller. There is no discussion agenda; it is just casual dialogue among a group of diverse team members sharing thoughts. So far, we haven't talked about work once! The discussion is lively and satisfying on both sides because we now know more about one another.

Professional: Be professional in every interaction regardless of the situation. People are much more receptive to feedback and direction when they feel there is an honest two-way dialogue occurring (feed back and forth). There are times, however, when staff just need to vent. I get it. That's the opportunity to let them know that what's said in the room stays in the room. I'm also okay with the occasional use of profanity or slang when blowing off some steam; it can be therapeutic before tackling the actual issue. In these instances, they ask for permission to talk freely, and I grant it. However, when we leave the room, it's back to handling the situation with complete professionalism. Having this open-door, free-spirit approach to unloading has improved the morale of the team and curbed some of the tension among staff.

Potential: Understand what the employee believes their potential is as a part of the team, in the department, and most importantly, as a part of the organization. Ask about their experience, both professionally and personally. Sometimes you have a set of skills available that weren't obvious due to the role that person currently holds. At one point, I inherited a team member, so her résumé was a long-gone artifact, and through discourse discovered that she was once a corporate lawyer. By mutual agreement, her role shifted from project manager to vendor management specialist overseeing our contracting efforts, which was actually in need of support. It was a good/better fit for all.

As a leader, I should be helping staff members reach their fullest potential. With my team, I push them to learn new skills and expand their experiences by cross-training them among all my functions. Understanding how others do their work and how it fits into the greater output is never wasted; it opens new doors, sparks innovative thinking, and may even breathe new life into a career.

Great example above of finding an individual's strengths and experiences and utilizing them!

Preference: Honor preferences but don't let them limit growth. Provide stretch assignments and safe audiences to help build skills and broadmindedness. This is actually where I hear the most thank-yous and see the most smiles.

Principles: I identify key principles for leading, such as demonstrating respect, using active listening, forgiving mistakes rather than harping on them, and being humble. These carry the responsibility of ensuring those around me feel comfortable and confident in our partnership. (And, as a side note, I've always thought the letter "P" resembles a person—a head with stick figure body—which reminds me of the human aspect of my job).

These valuable insights come from a successful Enlightened Manager who goes through her daily managerial responsibilities with great confidence and a clear conscience. Who wouldn't want to be on her team?

ATTRIBUTES OF AN ENLIGHTENED MANAGER

It's simple:
- Treat all people with the utmost respect.
- Have empathy.
- Be honest and sincere.
- Show appreciation.
- Build trust.
- Be fair.
- Mentor your staff.
- Have a positive influence.
- Go to bat for your people.
- Catch someone doing something right.
- Respect yourself.
- Be transparent.
- Share a common goal.
- Care about your employees.
- Be flexible.
- Don't jump to conclusions.
- Communicate positively and effectively.
- Make work fun.
- Give real praise and support.
- Don't play favorites.
- Provide a safe place for all.

If you follow these points, then the bumps in the road will be just that, bumps.

I have come across some truly gifted people in my career. The smart ones are confident enough not to try and show off how much they know. They have subtle self-confidence. Be confident in yourself as a human being; know that you don't mean harm to anyone, that you are here to build up not tear down. Coming from a good place will always lead you to a better place.

CHAPTER 4: GUIDING PRINCIPLES FOR AN ENLIGHTENED MANAGER

MANAGING A NEW DEPARTMENT

One thing that I never understood was how a new manager, in any given department, could act so arrogantly from day one about how this new (to them) place should be run. Yes, people are hired because of their expertise, but there are usually other solid staff members who have been part of the team for many years who have great insight into the organization. A new manager should always take the time to speak one-on-one with every single member of their new department. You should introduce yourself by telling them your story, then ask them theirs. Ask your staff members what their roles are, how long they've been with the organization, and then request their wish list for making their experience at work better. End the meet and greet by assuring them that you will always have an open-door policy with the whole office—and mean it. There's so much knowledge within one's midst; take advantage of it by engaging your staff from the start. Begin every single relationship with Respect, Empathy, Trust, and Transparency (RETT). If you follow this edict, you will build long-lasting, fruitful relationships.

At one of my favorite jobs, I managed a team of administrative assistants—who, by the way, are the backbone of any company, so please appreciate them. Prior to getting the job, my final interview was with one of the senior administrative assistants who would be reporting to me. If I won her over, I'd get the job. If not, I'd be out of luck.

After cordial introductions, she asked me right off whether I was planning on moving her to another location. It was obvious that this was causing her grief. This department had two locations in Southern California; my position was in one office and some of my staff were at the other location. I asked her if she wanted to be moved and she vehemently said no. I assured her that I was going to do all that I could to leave her right where she was. This gave her peace of mind. I got the job, and we went on to have a great working relationship.

Many times, when there is new management, there is angst. An Enlightened Manager will assure their inherited staff that they are there to make things better, not to cause turmoil or disruption.

RECRUITING/HIRING

ATTRIBUTES TO LOOK FOR:
CHARACTERISTICS OF GOOD EMPLOYEES

No matter what role you are looking to fill, these guidelines will help you get the best results.

Of course, you want to look for basic competence. Just as importantly, look for a positive attitude and great interpersonal skills. A positive attitude usually means that the candidate is flexible, not easily deterred, and is resourceful. People with great interpersonal skills work well with others, are good communicators, and will exert a positive influence on the team.

The most valued employees I have come across have been those who have been competent, reliable, resourceful, and dedicated. If you come across someone with these attributes, hire them and make sure to build on their natural momentum. It is a huge responsibility to take care of these great employees. If you lead well, you will have a whole team of these wonderful people and your futures will be limitless.

HIRING PROCESS

THE JOB POSTING

Make sure you provide the specifics of the job requirements, but don't list every single attribute that would make a perfect candidate. Nothing deters solid applicants more than an overtly long list of responsibilities on a job posting. Keeping the description a bit general will get you a larger pool of applicants to choose from. Many job seekers are scared off if they don't meet at least 90 percent of the requirements and won't even bother to apply if they don't reach this threshold. It's a balancing act; yes, you do need some very specific talents, but you don't want to limit your choices too narrowly either. We live in a very specialized world, but please also keep an open mind to those who may not have the exact requirements—they may be able to learn on the job and bring other attributes to the position, which will make them a great all-around hire. I believe well-roundedness and flexibility are excellent attributes for any candidate.

Take the time to review résumés (stop taking résumés after you have at least ten solid leads). Once you have a good pool of applicants, review qualifications thoroughly and start to categorize them by their abilities. I don't believe in "weeding" out applicants—looking for any reason not to hire them. I'd rather focus on those who have the best general attributes: education, experience, and skills. It's all in your outlook.

Hold face-to-face interviews. In our busy workdays, it may be difficult to schedule one-on-one interviews. Phone interviews are much easier, but they won't give you a real sense of whom you are dealing with.

Take the time to meet the qualified candidates in person. Hold two rounds, at most three, of interviews. In my opinion, the hiring manager, their boss, and possibly a colleague or a non-management staff should be more than enough to make a good decision. You don't want too many people having a say because you can't make everybody happy.

I once worked in a department where the process for hiring new staff was a gauntlet; multiple interviews were the norm. Every single team member had a say and, unfortunately, they were all quite paranoid, thinking that the robust candidates would quickly find better opportunities and leave after only a few months, or that some assertive applicants would become rabble-rousers. Sadly, some excellent candidates were disregarded because of these unnecessary interviewing obstacles placed in their way.

What seemed democratic became a subjective popularity contest. None of us are fortunetellers; we don't know how things are going to turn out from one day to the next. All one can do is try and hire the best overall candidates, period. As the hiring manager, do your due diligence, trust your instincts, and make an informed decision.

It is also very important to be positive, pleasant, and attentive with your candidates while interviewing them. You want to attract the best applicants, so you need to show them why they should want to work for you/your organization. Hiring is a two-way street. Always come prepared with questions and comments for every interview. I would send the interviewees a list of questions that they should be ready to discuss at least a couple of days before the actual interview. If you really want to hear the qualifications of an applicant, then give them some time to prepare their best answers. You want a well-thought-out reply, not an off-the-cuff response.

From your finalists, request at least three professional references. When you get this information, make sure to call each of them. This will give you a feel for the applicant's work ethic, interpersonal skills, and all-around competence.

One time, I was ready to hire a young man for a position, but after I called his last reference, I changed my mind. That reference wasn't very impressed by this applicant and told me that, given the chance, they would not work with him again. This was a major red flag, since he chose the reference without understanding where he stood with that person, so I moved on to the next candidate.

Lastly, please remember not to take too long to decide; good candidates will have other options. After everything checks out, make your decision, and celebrate it!

ON-BOARDING

Once you've chosen your awesome candidate and have agreed on a start date, make sure they have all the tools needed to begin on the right foot: clean cubicle/office, nameplate, telephone, computer, software, keys, ID, etc. It's very important that you provide your new hire with the essentials from the start. Introduce them to the entire staff on day one—have a quick team meeting for introductions, if possible. There's nothing worse for a new employee than sitting around on their first day totally lost with no direction. Make them feel welcomed and supported from the onset. Throughout this entire process, be transparent and build the trust that will be crucial for a successful longstanding union.

TRAINING

One of the most important lessons that stuck with me at UPS was that they hated firing people. They would always say that it costs money to on-board a new employee, and it would cost even more money to hire that person's replacement. They believed in training and retraining until an employee could successfully do the job. It is crucial to invest in giving your new staff member the time and resources to succeed. Create a solid training game plan with new hires and give them time to make mistakes and to learn from them. You want to make sure that your new staff members know exactly what is expected of them and how to perform their jobs from the onset.

Set aside a good amount of productive time to train them. I would say at least three months of solid training is required for most jobs. As their manager, you should be the driving force behind the plan, but you don't have to put the entire burden on yourself. Have others in the department who may do a similar job, or who may have had that role previously, sit down and do some training, too. Set up meet-and-greets with project stakeholders. Robust associations are crucial for any employee, so do all that you can to get these relationships on solid footing. At UPS, we had a training manual to log the day-to-day training. I'm not saying to follow this playbook, but you should form a solid plan for every new hire in every position. It will pay off.

The new hire should be allowed to ease into the full responsibilities of the job, a sort of grace period. Don't throw your new partner in the deep end right off the bat. If you do, you will risk them never truly getting a firm grip on what their job entails. Remember, train, train, and retrain all new employees. Every step should be carefully thought out to establish real confidence in your new staff members. Putting in the proper training time will allow their professional growth to take root much sooner.

I was once hired by a high-ranking executive director who was too busy to give me any hands-on training. He was based in Northern California (NCAL) and I was in Southern California. He was very up front with me about his limited time, so he paired me up with my counterpart from NCAL. She flew down for a couple of days to show me the ropes, but since I still needed more hands-on training, we connected through WebEx a couple of hours each day for two weeks straight. She went over every single duty with me and every single program I needed to familiarize myself with. I took meticulous notes, and once off WebEx, I'd immediately go over every single process she had taught me. If there were gaps, I'd write them down and ask about them at our next meeting. I must admit that I was at first leery about this training process, but it all worked out perfectly. My counterpart in NCAL knew her job to a tee and was patient, concise, and supportive all the way through. It was the best training I had ever received. So, it is crucial to have the appropriate training schedule/program implemented for all employees, no matter under what circumstances.

During this training period, make sure to have weekly check-ins to go over the trainings that have been conducted to see how your new person is taking it all in. Is it working? Are they learning? Are there any suggestions to improve the process? This is the time to put it all on the table for both of you.

It's also very important to have reasonable expectations. Yes, the recruit should have a basic knowledge of the job, but that person most likely doesn't know the full ins and outs of the position, or of your particular work environment. Be patient and fair from the inception. As your new team member grows, you will be able to entrust them with more responsibility, but don't overwhelm them at the start of your partnership. The main thing is to train and train until your new employee can fly on their own.

PERFORMANCE REVIEWS

Performance reviews should be a simple recap of the year. One question should be the basis of the review: did this team member perform their work optimally? Three specific topics should be covered:

- Aptitude
- Interpersonal skills
- Project management skills

The simpler the better.

I once worked for an international financial firm that handed out a twenty-page PDF to all its supervisors, managers, and directors on "how to conduct yearly reviews." When I got my copy, I immediately knew this place was not for me.

This same company held calibration meetings where they had other managers from across the country weigh in on staff review ratings, which meant that people who didn't know a particular staff member from Adam were dictating that person's rating. My high ratings of my best employees were overturned through this process, and it was infuriating. They purposely made it almost impossible for anyone to get an exceptional ranking, pushing everyone toward the middle instead. But year after year, managers played along with this farce.

It was completely irrational and a waste of time.

Unfortunately, many companies use performance reviews as an inquisition, a court trial where staff are put on the spot and must defend themselves against the prosecution. This causes much unnecessary stress and can turn off many solid employees. I've seen firsthand the angst that many employees feel during performance review time; I've felt it myself. One colleague put it this way: "Shouldn't my boss know how hard I work every day? Why do I have to prove it now by writing a thesis on it? Weren't my daily actions proof enough?"

Good, consistent work should be acknowledged and rewarded periodically. An Enlightened Manager knows the value of all their staff every single day and will be coaching and mentoring them throughout the year. There should be no surprises or pressure when reviewing the year with your team members. Performance review season should not be a stressful time. It should be a casual conversation between peers to discuss how the year went.

I'm also a big fan of 360 reviews. Managers should also be reviewed yearly on how they are managing their staff. It's only fair, in my opinion. Many organizations are dead set against this because they don't want to know the truth, which is unfortunate because people, at all levels, are the backbone of any business and their opinions should matter.

WHEN DEALING WITH AN UNCOOPERATIVE EMPLOYEE

An Enlightened Manager will always show respect and have the patience to develop solid trusting relationships, no matter how difficult it may seem. But there is a line that no one should cross. When someone is disrespectful and shows aggressive behavior, that line has been crossed. This comportment must be addressed and corrected immediately. There is no room for this type of treatment from anyone toward anyone.

In one situation, I had just started a new position where one of my direct reports was vehemently opposed to seeing me succeed. To this day, I still don't understand the animosity this person felt toward me. I had rough beginnings with new staff before, and I had always gained their full trust through graciousness and tenacity. This situation was different.

This staff member spread lies about me, undermined me at every chance, and was belligerent toward me in meetings. This was just unacceptable. Nonetheless, I approached the situation with the utmost care and dignity. I held weekly one-on-one meetings with this person, trying to get to the root of the problem and have it changed. I asked what I could do to make things better. Unfortunately, this employee never answered my questions, and instead continued with their insolent behavior toward me. It got to the point where I felt the need to involve HR in the matter. Down the road, this person did alter their poor attitude toward me and actually apologized for it.

An Enlightened Manager will know to deal with challenging scenarios with sensitivity and insight and to utilize the proper resources at hand to deal with them appropriately.

TEAM MEETINGS

I once reported to a manager who had no clue how to conduct effective and efficient team meetings. We'd all sit around staring at one another and waiting for him to talk. He never even put together a simple agenda. It was clear that he was merely going through the motions.

I found myself taking the lead by stepping in and actually running the meeting myself so that the staff got the information they needed and deserved. An Enlightened Manager will make a concerted effort to hold useful meetings where everyone is encouraged to ask questions and have time to discuss topics they deem important.

HOW TO CONDUCT EFFECTIVE MEETINGS

Meetings are an essential part of any business. They are used for project updates, announcements, strategizing, celebrations, business pitches, etc. Conducting effective meetings will not only help you stay connected with your staff and on top of your projects, but it will also save you time and effort.

- Team meetings should be held at least bimonthly.
- Try to schedule these meetings for the same day and time every week. This will help your staff avoid scheduling conflicts.
- Email meeting calendar invites as early as possible.
- Have an agenda, and email it to staff with enough time to receive comments or suggested changes.
- Start on time and limit the gathering to one hour or less.
- Everyone should be encouraged to participate.
- Ask for feedback about the meeting process.
- Alternate meeting coordinators.
- Have someone take meeting notes; use various members for this responsibility.
- Cancel meetings if there is not enough discussion material. Don't have a meeting merely to have it. You can email the team this information instead. Staff will be grateful for the time given back to them.
- Post meeting: Email meeting notes and ask for additions or

corrections within the following two days. Then highlight deliverables for the next meeting.

ONE-ON-ONES (1:1s)

Sincere 1:1s with individual members of your team are crucial. This is a great way to stay connected with them, to get project updates, and to brainstorm how to make things better. An Enlightened Manager knows the value of these get-togethers and will make them meaningful and constructive.

One director I reported to never missed our scheduled meeting, but after a while, it was obvious he was not truly listening to what I was saying at these meetings. Week after week, he would broach the same topics until one day I told him straight out that we had gone over this already and that I felt that he was not taking our time together seriously. There's nothing more frustrating than knowing your boss is not that interested in what you have to say.

In complete contrast, I deeply appreciated when a manager met with me, face-to-face or virtually, and I felt that we had discussed everything on our minds thoughtfully and productively.

TRULY BENEFICIAL ONE-ON-ONES

- Hold them biweekly on the same day and time. Half an hour to one hour should suffice but leave it up to your staff member to decide the actual length.
- Make sure both of you have topics to discuss and take notes.
- Always start off by checking in to see how things are going with your team member. An Enlightened Manager takes a real interest in their staff.
- Be open to discussing non-business topics. Your team member may need to inform you of some personal issues they may be

going through. An Enlightened Manager will always show empathy and offer help if needed.

- When the meeting ends, thank your team member for their time and make sure both of you follow up in a timely manner on queries.

Utilize 1:1s wisely; they are a great way to show that you care.

LEADERS KNOW HOW TO RALLY THE TROOPS

Two of the most crucial attributes of any employee are being resourceful and flexible. Many times, priorities shift from one minute to another. Occasionally, everything must be dropped to focus on a spur-of-the-moment major project. It's crunch time! That's when being resourceful and flexible pays off.

There were quite a few times at UPS where my team and I would be wrapping up our work only to hear that another team needed help finishing their workload before the other shift started. Without hesitation, I would send my crew to help put out that fire. Even though my staff was tired after a long night's work, I always expressed to them that we were part of a bigger team, so they were always up for the challenge. When we were under the gun, others would rally around us, too. Flexibility and generosity go a long way. You always get back what you give, so be giving.

CROSS-TRAINING

It is very important to cross-train as many of your staff as possible. People go on vacations, they go on personal leaves, they move on to other jobs. At every place I've worked, I always took the time to train my staff on some of my general responsibilities. So, when I was unavailable, for whatever reason, someone was there to take over for me seamlessly. If you don't cross-train, you will jeopardize your department's workflow and you may never fully recover.

BUILDING SYNERGY

A team comprises various personalities. An Enlightened Manager will bring all these individuals together to build synergy. In a perfect world, all your staff members would be best friends, but this is not usually the case. It is a manager's responsibility to, at the very least, create a professional and respectful work environment for the entire team. Your staff should clearly understand the common goals they share and how each member has a role in achieving those objectives. You should never pit members of your team against each other or play favorites. Treat them all fairly and equally. Do not ever allow gossip, finger pointing, undermining, or negativity to take hold in your office.

An Enlightened Manager will never tolerate this and will always make sure to provide their team with the most respectful, positive, and conducive work environment. Everyone should feel that they are vital to the team. When everybody feels vested, empowered, and heard, the possibilities are limitless.

COMMUNICATION/INTERPERSONAL SKILLS

It is simply horrible to show up to work every day dreading the next email that pops up on your screen from your manager. In one job I held, I would receive very aggressive and accusatory emails from my new manager. It was evident that this person was trying to make my life difficult. Not surprisingly, I didn't feel good about coming to work. There's nothing worse than feeling like your boss is gunning for you; it's unproductive, unnecessary, and unhealthy. At the very first meeting I had with this person, they stated that I had a misperception of how well I was performing my job. In other words, after years in which I had been doing this job with no issues whatsoever, with multiple successful evaluations, suddenly, according to this new manager, I was now not doing it correctly. This was news to me.

Right off the bat, I felt defensive and knew that this was not going to be an ideal situation for me.

As a manager, you set the tone for every single relationship you will have with your staff, so please be very conscious of your words and actions. You should always be mindful as to how you communicate with your team members. Always remember this quote from Maya Angelou:

> **"I've learned that people will forget what**
> **you said, people will forget what you did,**
> **but people will never forget how you**
> **made them feel."**

First, do not ever send aggressive, threatening emails/communications, period. This just causes stress, distrust, anger, and fear. If you would like to speak to an employee about something that may be an issue or may become one, it is always best to do it one-on-one and in a conference room instead of in your office. A room that's a bit larger and nicer sets a better tone than being called to the "principal's office."

You may also want to ensure that this is a private conversation, so holding it away from the main office space may work best. It is extremely important to keep in mind that you are having a straightforward conversation with another adult. So don't be accusatory, belittling, authoritarian, condescending, or aggressive. Be open, honest, and flexible.

State why you asked to speak to this individual in the first place, give your perspective, but then get their side of the issue. Take notes. Ask what can be done to make the situation better. Assure them that you want a positive resolution that will work for everyone. Is it workload? Is it a personality conflict? Or are a project's objectives unclear? Whatever the reason may be, make sure you are committed to a peaceful and positive resolution. Yes, I use the word peaceful because we all want peace in our lives. Bad managers breed a warlike environment: us against them. This is terribly unhealthy. No one wants to wake up every morning readying for battle.

The American Psychological Association estimates that more than $500 billion is siphoned off from the U.S. economy because of workplace stress, and 550 million workdays are lost each year due to stress on the job.

An Enlightened Manager will be willing to try different things to make the relationship work. If you must reassign a task, change processes, add staff to a project, or re-train the team, do it. Be creative, be innovative, have compassion, show empathy. Assure this employee that you are committed to taking away any obstacles that may be impeding this person's road to success. If your team knows you have their back under any circumstance, they will trust in you and they will have your back, too, through thick and thin.

WORKING THINGS THROUGH!

At another organization where I once worked, Mari, an administrative assistant who reported to a fellow manager, was put on a performance improvement action plan for allowing some of her important tasks to slip through the cracks. The director of that department, whom Mari supported, felt that the situation was serious enough to place her on this improvement strategy. Action plans at this organization were usually seen as a final warning before firing an employee. They were not actually utilized as "improvement plans" as they were supposed to be, so many employees dreaded them.

In this instance, my fellow manager assured me that she just wanted to make sure Mari got better in her role. Mari was of course upset; she felt that her days were numbered at this job. She began just going through the motions, not really putting any effort into addressing the issues brought to her attention. My management colleague asked me if I could speak to Mari, since we had worked on a couple of projects together and had a good working relationship. I agreed.

I met with Mari away from the office at a café to discuss the situation. I told her that contrary to what she may have thought, her manager actually wanted her to get better at her role and had no intention of firing her. This was what her manager had conveyed to me. From our previous interactions, Mari trusted me and was put at ease after we spoke.

I went over the action plan with Mari and gave her detailed advice as to how to tackle these tasks. I also told her to feel free to reach out to me anytime if she needed any help. After our discussion, Mari's attitude completely changed, and I'm proud to say that she passed this trial period with flying colors and remained with the organization with an improved performance. It was a win-win situation.

Always coach and support your team, be honest and up front with them; you are there to help them achieve their potential, not to set them up for failure.

BUILDING TRUST: GETTING TO THE ROOT OF IT

If there are some serious issues being exposed, get in there and communicate openly with your team: don't be afraid of what you may find, don't get all your information from a select few (they may be biased), be open to everyone's concerns. Those who are truly interested in having a strong, resourceful, successful, and dedicated staff need to gain every single one of their team members' trusts, not just the ones they "like."

A GOOD THING TO REMEMBER:

Respect leads to Trust.
Trust leads to Loyalty.
Loyalty leads to Dedication.
Dedication leads to Innovation.
Innovation leads to success all around.

CONFLICT RESOLUTION:
RESOLVING DISAGREEMENTS AMONG TEAM MEMBERS WITH GRACE AND DISCERNMENT

When issues arise, especially due to personality conflicts, I honestly feel that if all parties concerned come from a good place, and are willing to treat each other as adults, then everything can be worked out cordially.

There were two employees in one of my departments (one of them was my direct report) who were having issues. They worked together daily; their jobs were interdependent. If one didn't do her part, then both their projects were in jeopardy.

The first thing I did was schedule a meeting for all three of us. I told them to be prepared to honestly discuss their grievances. When we met, there was tension in the air. I started the conversation by saying that both of them were good, respectful, hardworking people and that I saw no reason this issue could not be worked out. This simple, honest, and empathetic statement put them at ease.

We went over the issues for an hour and came up with solutions that all were happy with. Soon they became comfortable with one another and eventually became great colleagues. They no longer needed a third party (management) involved for any conflicts; from then on, they worked out their differences between each other. We're all human beings; we all make mistakes, so we shouldn't be so hard on each other. Everything can be worked out peacefully if we're open to it.

TAKE GOOD CARE OF ALL OF YOUR STAFF ("POOL THE TALENT")

EVERYONE BRINGS SOMETHING TO THE TABLE

Tailor, accommodate, and be flexible in your day-to-day interactions with your individual employees, especially with the hardworking ones in the background who may not get all the glory.

On almost every team, there will be staff working on some "important projects," the bread and butter of the department. At the same time, other employees not involved with the "sexy" projects help keep the place running day to day. Many times, the "high-profile" employees get all the attention and accolades. Please keep in mind that you need to be there for all your team members. They all bring something to the table, and you are responsible for all their well-being. It's your duty to bring out the very best in all of them, providing an environment that will allow them to fulfill their potential. When staff members are working optimally, you will clearly see the results. It is very important to acknowledge every team member's role and worth.

A good practice is to have various personnel periodically give a brief presentation on what they do to the rest of the staff. This will give everyone a view into their colleagues' daily contributions. Many times, people are surprised to find out how other departments work. They're so caught up in their own projects that they never take the time to completely understand the everyday logistics that it takes to run an office. An Enlightened Manager understands that everybody brings something to the table and deeply appreciates every single one of their staff.

VIOLA'S STORY

I once knew an employee who was hardworking, resourceful, and very knowledgeable about the entire department. She wasn't outgoing or showy and she sometimes had issues interacting with fellow employees—she could be "moody." After a rough start (she was standoffish with me, too), I got to know her well. She turned out to be a very interesting, kind, ethical, and even funny person. It was a real joy getting to know who she really was. Her immediate manager wrote her off as a bad apple because some of the staff complained about her supposed "negative attitude." Of course, having a negative attitude doesn't quite come to mind when one thinks of good employees. But there may be a legitimate reason behind this behavior. Look into it. A good manager never jumps to conclusions.

Viola just wanted to be treated fairly, she wanted to be recognized, and she wanted to be compensated adequately. She had felt that her manager treated some staff better than others, and she may have had a point.

Viola was crucial to the department but was not in a high visibility position; nonetheless, she was doing a great job day in and day out, in the background. She was getting critical daily projects done with little recognition or support. Unfortunately, after not being recognized for her immense contributions to the organization, Viola left for another job. The staff had been unaware of the many, many nuts and bolts that Viola was quietly taking care of daily. The office was lost without her and everyone was now scrambling to fill that void. An Enlightened Manager will always know and appreciate the contributions of all their team members.

I stayed in touch with Viola, and she confided in me that all she ever wanted was fair compensation for her contributions, but more importantly, she wanted to be positively acknowledged occasionally. What an unnecessary loss for this organization. As a manager, you need to value each of your staff's work and contributions and reward them accordingly. Not everyone is happy-go-lucky; some are quiet, private people. This is okay. Individualize your management style to each member of your team.

A good manager always acknowledges hard work, dedication, and loyalty without being asked. It doesn't always have to be a financial reward. It is your responsibility as a manager to know your staff's contributions and to acknowledge them adequately. I understand that we live in a society that rewards the "shiniest" people, but let us never forget the quiet, hardworking, dedicated people that are the backbone of any organization, those who get the work done day in and out in the shadows. Without them, we'd be completely lost.

"THE MINUTIAE ARE EXCRUCIATING"

I was once part of a department that was crucial to the overall well-being of an entire organization. The problem was that the person in charge was obsessed with every minor detail. This director's brand was "perfection." This person had convinced the executives in charge that that was the way things had to be, so this administrator burdened staff with these unreasonable expectations.

The team had to deal with the back and forth of getting every minor detail right for every single task, causing them to feel stressed, overworked, and frustrated. One veteran employee described her frustration with the situation by saying that the "minutiae in the department was excruciating." The turnover rate was high, and the remaining team members were always looking to get out. Do not bog down your staff with minutiae or unnecessary work. Keep your eye on their bigger, overall contribution, and stay focused on that. I like to say that it doesn't have to be perfect, just done very well.

This same manager also inundated certain team members with tons of work, while others had minimal projects and were always out the door hours earlier than the rest of the team. There was obviously a disproportional alignment of the workload. It seemed that this boss was not treating everyone equally.

As a manager, it is crucial that you know how to manage workflow and assignments. An Enlightened Manager will treat direct reports equitably, especially when it comes to distributing job responsibilities and the offering of fringe benefits. Always work smart and fair.

SHOW EMPATHY

EMPATHY! EMPATHY! EMPATHY! As a leader, you must have and show empathy to every single one of your employees. To be truly effective, you must be able to place yourself in their shoes. Once you're able to see things from their vantage point, you'll much more effectively get to the root of many issues, leading to viable solutions to many problems. Remember: treat others the way you'd like to be treated. There's nothing worse than working for an unsympathetic manager, especially when you may be going through some personal issues.

AUTONOMY

Be a partner with your staff, not an authoritarian—give them autonomy. Trust them, guide them only if need be. Form partnerships with your team. We are all capable adults, so we should treat each other as such.

The best job I ever had was as an administrative supervisor in the marketing department for a large healthcare organization. My managers throughout my stint there were always professionally respectful. They were serious business professionals who knew their stuff; they were never disrespectful or rude.

One of the things that kept me happy and motivated was the autonomy I was given. I had brief weekly check-in calls with my boss just to make sure everything was good, and we'd have monthly staff meetings for team cohesion and informational purposes. But day-to-day, I was left alone to do my job as I thought best. They showed confidence in my ability to perform my responsibilities. Because of this environment, we all excelled, we had confidence in one another's talents, and we were always coming up with better ways of doing things. This was the environment that existed; independence was the driving force.

Give your staff room to perform their jobs without questioning their every move and motives. I'll just say it! Don't micromanage your people. Micromanagers get so caught up in everyone else's jobs that they are never able to focus on the bigger picture: leading their departments to their full potential. Autonomy breeds confidence and innovation at every turn.

BUILD UP PEOPLE'S STRENGTHS AND PASSIONS

Utilize their talents! Don't bog down employees with tasks they don't enjoy and won't thrive while doing. I'm not referring to their major job responsibilities but rather other rudimentary tasks that they may have picked up along the way. As a manager, it is your duty to make sure your staff is being utilized for their talents. You must study them to see who is good at what projects and which staff would enjoy other tasks. This takes intellect. Too many managers just see black and white: "I can assign you whatever I see fit. I'm in charge." Enlightened Managers are nuanced thinkers, not simple-minded people.

At one of my jobs, I put a team together for an assignment that needed to be completed in one week. It was my fault for not jumping on it sooner, but nonetheless, the project still had to get done. I took accountability by apologizing to this newly formed group for the late start and offered my full support to them.

Off the bat, there was one person I was concerned about. Sharon had been in the military and was a seasoned professional. She was outspoken but always sincere. I knew she was extremely busy and that she wasn't going to be happy about being recruited for this project. I knew I had to be sensitive to her concerns.

I immediately sent the team an email explaining the project's mission and came up with a quick but solid game plan. I then set up a meeting for the newly formed group. Sharon jumped right in; she had a great idea about how to execute the project. I got the group's consensus, and we all agreed on pursuing her plan, and I dropped my initial concept. The fact that you're the boss doesn't mean you always have the best ideas. Be open to others' thoughts and develop the talents they have to offer. Sharon stepped up and helped lead the project.

We hashed out the presentation for the project through e-mail and met two more times within the next few days. The result was informative, well received, and a success.

After the assignment was completed, we discussed our short but productive journey. Sharon told us that in a previous job, which she really loved, she was a professional development trainer and that this short project gave her a chance to sharpen those old skills. She was quite elated about it all. Sharon also stated that she appreciated how I took the reins—picking a particular path, moving quickly, and empathetically taking all their busy schedules into consideration. This is a great example of how to manage by utilizing your team's passions, talents, and time. You just have to set the right tone, ask the right questions, be flexible, and take a sincere interest in others. The results will amaze you. Lead!

AN ENLIGHTENED MANAGER IS ALWAYS UP FRONT AND HONEST

I once hired an assistant, and I must openly admit that I made a mistake doing so. She wasn't the best qualified, but she had stated that she really needed the job, so I gave her a chance. I felt that with some close supervision and coaching, she would be fine. As I worked with her, I realized that she couldn't carry out the basic elements of the position. It turned out that she was lacking elementary interpersonal skills and experience. I gave her hands-on training, gave her specific instructions and timeframes, but nothing seemed to work. It had gotten to the point that she was not contributing to the effectiveness of the department whatsoever. My own job was suffering because I was spending so much time looking after her work.

After three months of rigorous training, I sat her down and explained to her that she wasn't a good fit and that we were letting her go. Of course, she was upset to hear this, as anyone would be about losing his or her job. But she thanked me for the time I had spent coaching her and trying to make it work. She acknowledged that she, too, realized that it wasn't a good fit.

This person was the only employee that I ever had to let go. I shouldn't have hired her in the first place—my fault completely. But I was open and honest through the whole process; I never led her to believe that everything was fine. There were no surprises. Being transparent and honest at every turn will gain you respect from your staff, under any circumstance.

NO NEED FOR "DIFFICULT CONVERSATIONS"

As managers, we're often trained by HR consultants on how to have "difficult conversations" with staff members. The premise for holding these "difficult conversations" is to tell employees that they are not doing their jobs, that they're being written up, or that they are being let go. As I have said before, trust is crucial for any successful, long-standing relationship. An Enlightened Manager will build real trust with their team. So, there will never be a need to have "difficult conversations." If changes need to be made or issues arise, these will merely be conservations among human beings. Both parties involved will trust one another enough to know they come from a sincere, well-intentioned place no matter the outcome.

PICK YOUR BATTLES. DON'T NITPICK. ALWAYS KEEP YOUR FOCUS ON THE BIG PICTURE.

At this same job, I had hired a temporary worker for the summer. She was a law student on break, and she quickly became an amazing employee. She learned her job almost instantly and made some long-lasting improvements to the office. People enjoyed working with her, and I never had to worry about the quality of her work, which made my life much easier. If there was one flaw, it was that she was late every single morning. Nonetheless, she was still very reliable; she actually never missed a day of work. I didn't see her tardiness as a major issue. She was not only getting her job done, but she was also constantly going above and beyond. I knew that a person this talented had a lot of options, and I wanted to hang on to her as long as possible. Once the summer was over, I hated to see her go, but she had other aspirations in life.

At her last-day luncheon, she expressed how much she had enjoyed working for me and that she had learned a lot from us. But she was curious about one thing: why had I never reprimanded her for being late every morning? I told her that she was such an exceptional employee that her tardiness wasn't an issue for me (it was not affecting the office's daily operations whatsoever) and that her positive contributions overwhelmingly outweighed her late mornings.

Don't sweat the small stuff; always have the bigger picture in mind. Keep things in context. Sometimes an employee can have a huge impact on an organization even if they have a short stint with you. Quality versus quantity.

POSITIVE WORK ENVIRONMENT

As a manager, it is your obligation to create and maintain a positive, productive, and professional work environment, to make staff feel content and even proud of their jobs. Corrupt office politics, gossip, meddling, favoritism, harassment, retaliation—none of these should ever be tolerated. These are all traits of a dysfunctional atmosphere and are a huge impediment to your staff and organization's well-being. As a manager, you must lead by example. Do not partake, condone, or simply ignore dishonorable behavior. You set the tone, so assure your team that you will always try to do the right thing. Then do it!

If you can create this type of workplace, your team will always work hard, be creative, and be results-driven. In complete contrast, if you create a hostile, distrustful, and negative office environment, your staff will feel no loyalty to you. You will eventually find yourself reaping what you sow; the universe will eventually catch up to you. Always treat folks right!

BUILD UP, DON'T TEAR DOWN

I once had a boss who would criticize new employees: he doesn't seem dedicated, she's not assertive enough, he's too loud, she doesn't seem to be catching on, etc. It was like clockwork. This boss wanted everyone to be a clone. This person would never give young, new employees the chance to really grow and prove themselves. They were stunted. I took it upon myself to keep this negative vibe from the newcomers. I always saw their potential, and it was my duty to build on it.

I had hired some young talent and I was training and mentoring them, but the work environment at this place was negative—gossip, meddling, and throwing folks under the bus was part of the daily routine. I had two direct reports and an intern. As a mid-level manager, I could only do so much to influence that department. I did what I could, but after a while, I saw that the negativity, lack of vision, gossip, and disrespect was not going to change. It kept getting worse.

While I was at this place, I tried my very best to instill in my team a sense of purpose, establish a safe space, and teach them skills that they could use anywhere they happened to find themselves in the future. I taught them how to utilize their strengths, how to be resourceful, how to work as a team, how to start a project, how to define it, how to gather vital information, how to follow up, and how to deliver. My goal is to always have a good influence on my staff and leave them a positive, long-lasting impression. As a manager, whether you have a team of two or two hundred, your main priority is your staff's well-being and getting the work done. Help your employees thrive under any condition.

LET YOUR STAFF FLY, AND FALL, AND FLY AGAIN

An Enlightened Manager will always take you to a better place, to the next level. They are someone who has vision, is creative, and knows how to implement long, impactful change. They will know how to achieve this on their own. Yes, some procedures are already in place that have proven successful. If it's not broken, no need to fix it. But sometimes a fresh pair of insightful eyes can see that even long-time successful processes can be improved. An Enlightened Manager will never shoot down solid ideas. They will be open and give honest feedback about all of them. An environment of free-flowing thoughts should be practiced every day.

I have experienced shortsighted directors—managers of managers—who were so caught up on rudimentary tasks that they stifled all creativity and growth. This should never be the case. All "leaders" in any organization should be big-picture thinkers. Another director hired me because he was looking for a big-picture thinker and stated that he was hoping for a partnership, rather than the supervisor/subordinate prototype. He was looking for someone who was going to take his department to a whole new place. This manager was a very busy executive but was always available to meet with me. We had a long-standing one-hour meeting every Thursday. Yes, he wanted ideas, but he also wanted them implemented. He made it clear that he was there to give insight, support, and advice.

This director's team had been in place for many years, and they were successful and were accustomed to a daily routine, but this boss of mine didn't want a master of tasks. Yes, he wanted me to learn all the daily duties the staff performed, and to be able to jump in and get my hands dirty, but more importantly, he wanted me to lead. This boss let me fly, and even when I fell, he let me fly again. He also always showed enthusiasm and passion toward the line of work we were performing. Positivity and enthusiasm go a very long way; it can be contagious. So having this enlightened attitude with your staff will make them strive for more and bring great results.

INTERNSHIPS AND MENTORING

One intern working for me was a young man who was entering his senior year in college. He was personable, reliable, and hardworking. It was a nine-week internship. After week two, my boss wanted to know whether I could cancel the internship; my manager wasn't happy with the student's progress up to that point. I wasn't about to do such a thing.

To this day, I don't think that boss fully understood what internships entail. Interns are there to learn, not to be gophers, so treat them with patience and respect—mentor them. They are the future, so please have a good, positive impact on them.

A few weeks later, after working with this intern on developing his professional and interpersonal skills, he had grown. He learned how to become an asset to an organization, how to navigate the office, and how to collaborate with a diverse staff. His internship paid off. My manager was subsequently impressed with his growth and contributions. My boss told the intern that he had received some great, solid mentoring from me, that he was getting real-world project management training for free.

Having a long-term vision, training, and a positive work environment holds great value. This intern was proof that this works. Please invest time and effort in young minds. One of the aspects of management that I most cherish is helping develop new talent and giving them lessons they can use for a lifetime. MENTOR! MENTOR! MENTOR!

LETTERS OF RECOMMENDATIONS/REFERENCES

An Enlightened Manager will always be happy when their staff members move up to better opportunities. I've been asked many times to be a reference or to write a recommendation letter for folks with whom I've worked throughout the years. I am happy to state that many of my colleagues have notified me that my remarks made a difference in landing new jobs. This is something that I am very proud of in my career. Be there for people throughout their journeys.

RELATIONSHIP BUILDING

Throughout my career, I have always gotten things done. I have been able to connect with people on a very human level, and most have loved working with me. I treat everyone special, with respect, the way I was raised to do.

Everything in life is about building good, solid relationships. This takes time and effort, but it pays off, and it's the right thing to do. Enlightened Managers are relationship builders. They create solid bridges with all they encounter on a daily basis. They interact positively with their staff, with the water delivery people, with their colleagues, and with their bosses. My point is that everyone plays a role, so develop good working relationships with everyone you meet throughout your day.

Everywhere I've worked, I have taken a sincere interest in every single person I dealt with. That is why the housekeeping folks were always willing to clean up my department with extra care, why outside vendors gave me discounts on the services they provided us, why Accounts Payable and Payroll expedited my requests when needed, why IT always fixed my tech issues ASAP, why other staff members were always willing to jump in and help when I needed them. It's all about relationships! Be good to others, and they will be good right back to you.

SHOW COURAGE, HAVE COMPASSION

CARMEN'S STORY

One of my best employees ever was this young person who, at the onset, did not have the perfect experience I was looking for. But through her résumé, I could see that she had the basic competencies to at least qualify for an interview. When she came in to meet with me, she was professional, respectful, and motivated. I could see that she was ready for the right break. I hired her soon afterward.

This job was a temporary position at an organization that offered decent pay and good benefits to its full-time/permanent staff. Contract employees didn't receive medical benefits, paid time off, or holiday pay, but many used these temporary positions to get their foot in the door. Carmen was no different. She knew that if she did well, she'd get a shot at a full-time job with us. She hit the ground running.

Carmen was extremely resourceful, and with every passing day, she was learning the company's systems and culture. Even though she was not a permanent employee, she became my best worker. A year later, we had a full-time opening, and I offered it to her. She deserved it.

During the hiring process for the permanent position, it came out that Carmen did not have a high school diploma as she had claimed on her temporary agency application. All employees in this organization were required to have at least a diploma. Carmen came clean with our HR department during the vetting process. She stated that her temp agency had told her to put down that she had a high school diploma in order to get the temporary assignment. Unfortunately, this put an immediate hold on her full-time employment aspirations. She apologized profusely for the misstep and stated that she was in the process of earning her GED.

My director was not pleased; in his eyes, her misrepresentation should have been reason enough to disqualify her from any employment with us. But he ultimately left the decision up to me.

From day one, Carmen had been an exemplary employee; she had become my go-to person. I trusted in her capabilities, and I relied on her. In my mind, she had earned a full-time position with us. None of us are perfect; we all make mistakes, and sometimes we just need a break.

I spoke to our HR department and told them that I still wanted to proceed with hiring Carmen permanently. We found a compromise, deciding to put her application on hold until she received her high school diploma equivalent.

Six months later, Carmen earned her GED as promised and became a permanent employee with health benefits, paid time off, holiday pay, and a decent salary. She earned and received the break she deserved. This is one of the things I am most proud of in my career as a manager. I helped someone who needed it. As a manager, don't be rigid—be open, be flexible, and always take good care of your employees. Be willing to take a stand for what you believe in. Always have the courage to do the right thing!

PROJECT MANAGEMENT 101:

CASE STUDY # 1 – GETTING IT DONE!

One of the most important qualities of an Enlightened Manager is the ability to successfully complete projects with professionalism, enthusiasm, and collaboration. This talent is crucial for any leader.

I was once assigned a training project that needed to be completed in one month. The first thing I did was get the relevant information/purpose of the event. I studied the information repeatedly until I knew exactly what had to be conveyed and accomplished on that day. I also got a budget from our vice president. I then recruited one of my staff to help, and I sent out a notice to the entire department asking for volunteers.

You always need to work with a good team on bigger projects. You can't and shouldn't try to do everything yourself—know when and how to delegate. The next thing I did was pick a date and time for the event. I sent out a Save the Date invite so that all who needed to attend could block off the time in their calendars. A date and time should be locked down ASAP for any event to give people enough time to fill in their calendars.

From the invite, I was also able to get an approximate head count from the reply/accept log. Aside from the date and time, the invite also included the purpose of the occasion. People need to know why they should attend or participate in the events you are putting together. It is also important that your audience have a stake in what you're promoting, or a buy-in. For this occasion, the staff was assured that this was going to be a day in which they were the focus and that it was going to be enjoyable and informative.

I had one of my staff who dabbled in graphic art design a colorful flyer with the event information. You must sell your projects, so I made the ad for the event appealing and inviting. Proper messaging is a big part of everything you do daily. Be a good communicator!

The next thing I did was lock down a location. It is important to have a proper venue secured ASAP. If you wait too long, the right locales will be booked, and you'll be stuck with a subpar site. I then put together a rough agenda to share with my vice president so she could get a sense of what I was planning, and so I could have a working outline. She promptly approved of my vision, and I continued.

Next on my list was to order a great meal. People always appreciate good food, especially when they're going to spend their lunch break working. I looked over several options and picked one that I felt appealed to most of our staff. I chose a menu that was also vegetarian friendly so most would enjoy the food. It's important to know that you will never completely satisfy everyone. You should shoot for an 80 to 90 percent satisfaction rate. If you try to make everyone completely happy, you may never get past first base. This lunch order is a case in point.

I contacted the vendor and ordered the lunches, also sooner rather than later. Whatever you can lock down early, do so immediately. I then looked for some interesting gifts/giveaways for the participants that would not break the bank. I picked a remote cellular phone charger in different bright colors; I knew this was something that most people could use. The original price online was $15 a piece, but after speaking to the sales manager, I got it down to $10 a piece. It was a bulk purchase, and the sales manager hoped that I'd order more from his company in the future. I also wanted to include a nice treat, so I ordered Chicago-style popcorn at a group discount rate, as well. The gift bag had something useful and fun for everyone, and I got it all for a very good price. Building relationships every step of the way is crucial toward reaching your goals. This was the case here when I dealt with outside vendors. Everything counts!

A few folks answered my call for volunteers, so I quickly recruited them. The committee now comprised four people. Jim was an experienced project manager, Brian and Raquel were new to the work world but full of creativity and enthusiasm, and Denise also had a project management background. I made sure to utilize their talents and experiences to the fullest.

From the onset, I was very respectful of everyone's time; we were all still expected to stay on top of our regular duties while working on this project. I met with them only a few times in person and for no more than an hour. I came into each meeting with a tight agenda, knowing exactly what needed to be covered, assigned, and followed up on. I sent out calendar invites and notes on what we needed to go over at our gatherings, so we'd all come prepared. This should be done for every meeting—go in with a plan so you don't waste anyone's valuable time.

The training day schedule included presentations, guest speakers, videos, stretch breaks, an icebreaker, and a teambuilding event. I assigned Jim to take care of the icebreaker and teambuilding event. He was a seasoned project manager and was very comfortable speaking in public. I knew he'd take care of business.

Meanwhile Brian, Denise, and Raquel helped come up with a theme and design for the event, which was a big part of the program. The "theme team," as they became known, developed into an independent entity; they planned their own meetings and didn't have to include me. This gave me time to focus on other things. Always delegate the right assignments to the right people, utilizing their individual talents for the common cause.

It is also crucial not to micromanage when you assign the right people the right assignments. Let them do their thing. Yes, check in on them to make sure they're on target and to see if they need any assistance. But we're all professionals, so we should always treat each other that way. We put together teams for a reason.

There are things that you should take care of yourself—the big-ticket items like costs that will affect the budget: venue, catering, supplies, guest speakers, videos, presentations, etc. Delegating is a beautiful thing, but only if there's true independence and trust. There's a big distinction between delegating and passing the buck. Delegating is smart and strategic while passing the buck is just plain old laziness.

I asked everyone what support they needed to complete their tasks. Jim was okay, and the theme team needed some basic office supplies to put together the day's motif. They gave me their list and I ordered it right away. When your team asks for resources, procure them ASAP.

It is good practice to have everyone involved in a project on the same page. One afternoon, I took the committee on a scouting trip to the event's location. We needed to know how to arrange the room, what technical set up was warranted—projector, laptop, speakers, video screens, internet access, etc. We also scouted the area to see how we were going to decorate it. While there, we had the location's audio-visual expert show us how to use the media equipment. Some venues will take care of this for you, but if they don't, you'd better know how to use the equipment yourself. You don't want to lose momentum by not knowing how to work a projector.

We tied up many loose ends on this excursion. For example, I also showed the facilities folks how we wanted the tables, chairs, and screens arranged. You may have to set up the space yourselves, so give yourself enough time for this, too.

Through it all, I kept a checklist to track what needed to get done and by when. I also made sure that the vendors knew how important it was to get the items I ordered in a timely manner. They all came through with flying colors. It's all about planning and timing.

I recruited the guest speakers early on, making sure that they would be available. It's a good idea to lock down keynote participants right away, as well.

There was someone we wanted to speak at the event. I contacted him immediately, but unfortunately, he was going to be out of the country at the time, so I went to plan B and found another presenter. Always be flexible and have a backup strategy. I then sat down with all the guest speakers to go over the purpose of their talks. I asked them to send me their presentations no later than three days before the event and to let me know if they were going to need anything from our end. The speakers I finally recruited were all self-sufficient; they didn't ask for anything from us and simply brought flash drives with their presentations on them. We just had to plug and play.

Our supplies and gifts arrived a week before the occasion. The next day, the entire planning committee got together to fill the gift bags and go over last-minute details. I made it into a laid-back afternoon with a nice lunch included. Give your team some easy time in the middle of a stressful assignment; they will appreciate it. During this period, I also checked in on the catering to make sure that they had all the pertinent information—order, time, and location. Follow up is crucial so you can avoid surprises.

Everything was coming together.

On the day of the event, I requested the team arrive two hours early to have enough time to set up. I also recruited another staff member to run the tech piece—laptop, microphones, videos, presentations, etc. I had previously trained him how to set up for these events, so he was a cool, calm pro now. We were ready to go.

I am very proud to say that everything went extremely well. The vendors came through, the decorations looked great, the icebreaker and team exercise were well received, and the speakers all had impactful presentations. As expected, there were a few hiccups. Be flexible and ready to troubleshoot. One of the presenters was running behind, so I had to change the agenda a bit. No worries—she showed up late but still delivered. The whole department enjoyed the event and appreciated the effort we put into making this day special. All our hard work paid off.

I made sure to introduce my team and thanked them several times throughout the day. They all came through and received great exposure to our leadership. It was a win-win for all of us. Remember, when someone wins, it doesn't mean that someone else has to lose. Be happy for those who shine.

There's this old deodorant commercial with the slogan "Never let them see you sweat." This is very true. Even though a great deal of background work goes into all projects, do your homework, stay cool, and keep your eye on the prize. If you put in the effort, it will look easy, even though we all know the hard work that it took.

Looking back on this project, I can reflect on how I got it done: Prepare! Prepare! Prepare! Logistics! Logistics! Logistics!

- Once I received the assignment, I immediately got the essential information and started working on it ASAP.
- I studied the material over and over—what was the objective, what was needed.
- I worked with a team; there was no way I could have done this myself.
- I had a checklist that I went over daily to see where we were at and what was needed.
- I had deadlines that I met, knew what needed to get done sooner than later in order to move on.
- I locked down event, date, time, and location.
- I utilized my team's talents and trusted their judgment. Give your staff autonomy.
- I prepped and followed up until the morning of the event. Leave no stone unturned.

- I made it fun and easy-going for the team and was always respectful of them and their time.
- I was flexible and moved on to plan B when needed.
- I was grateful for my team, and I acknowledged them publicly for their contributions.

The main thing I did was focus on logistics, logistics, logistics. I don't call it being detailed oriented. You can get too caught up in trying to be perfect; paying too much attention to every little detail can easily distract you from the bigger picture. I am always much more focused on logistics than being consumed by every minor aspect.

This is how I was successful in this event. I hope you can take something valuable from this example and use it to accomplish your own projects.

PROJECT MANAGEMENT CASE STUDY # 2 – MAKING *PAN DULCE Y CHOCOLATE*

After finishing graduate school in Miami, Florida, I immediately moved to Los Angeles to try and make movies. I didn't know a soul in LA at the time, but I knew it was where I needed to be. Aside from shooting a few short videos in graduate school, I had never made a movie before. The first thing I did was connect with like-minded folks who shared my vision. I was blessed that I immediately connected with someone who eventually became my best friend and whom I now actually consider family. She shared my vision of the movie I wanted to make, so we tackled this huge project together.

Adriana had never made a movie before either, but we both knew how to get things done. I pulled everything I had learned from film school, my past jobs, and personal experiences to make this happen. We had no money; we had to rely on pure passion to get people to donate funds, time, talent, and services to our cause. We had to recruit talented film personnel who would be willing to contribute to our little movie. Through sheer kindness and generosity from many, many people, we were able to raise a few thousand dollars to make *Pan Dulce y Chocolate*. This wasn't a sizeable budget by any means, but it was just enough.

A great deal goes into making a movie. The pre-production stage takes a lot of meetings and planning. Production—which is the actual shooting schedule—can take several long days. Post-production is the editing and making sure everything flows and looks and sounds good. All these elements take an equally great deal of time and effort. Every step of our journey had to be meticulously planned out and executed; since most services were donated, we had to be very conscious of people's time and talents. We had to be extremely organized: equipment rental deadlines, locking down locations, shooting schedules, and so forth.

There were a few main skills that helped us put this huge project together on a minimal budget:

Research: We were novices at this. We had to research how to make a movie, find shooting locations, recruit personnel, rent equipment, find talent.

Logistical skills: Meetings, shooting schedules, locations, auditions, catering; it was all about logistics.

Tenacity: We were determined to make this short film, so we figured it all out.

Great interpersonal skills: Both Adriana and I sold our project to anyone who would listen. We were able to raise funds and recruited a very talented cast and crew. We received freebies from food vendors, production houses, business owners, and studio lots. People saw our sincerity and passion and were willing to help us out. Building solid relationships was crucial.

Budgeting/financial acumen: We had minimal funding that had to go a very long way. We wanted to pay all our staff for their talent and time, but we just couldn't. Our cast and crew were amazing; they believed in our project, so they donated their talent and time to us. We saved our money for things that were crucial and that we couldn't get comped, like equipment and editing costs. We were able to get these services heavily discounted, but we still had to pay for them.

We were organized, trying our best not to waste anyone's valuable time. We also gave our team timely breaks and meals; we didn't want to burn them out and overstress them. We were thankful for all their hard work, thanking them at every turn and sticking to our promise of making this a positive experience.

It was an amazing journey. All the details about how we pulled it off are beyond the scope of this book. What I want to emphasize here is the management aspect of it all. We had to completely understand the magnitude of our task. We had to manage a very tight budget. We had to recruit talent and services. We had to sell our idea and ourselves. We had to keep staff motivated (without pay) and happy.

We were always completely respectful to all of them, even when we were under the gun to wrap up before the equipment had to be returned (we'd be charged higher rates if late), or before we had to vacate a donated location, or before the talent had to go to a paying gig. We worked around both our and their needs. Through it all, I'm glad to note, the cast and crew looked forward to coming in and working with us every day. They all said that it was a wonderful experience for them.

My producing partner and I were very proud when we completed the movie. We were showcased at a few film festivals across the country and the movie also played on a local Los Angeles TV station at three o'clock on an early Wednesday morning. What started out as a dream had become a reality!

It took great management skills to achieve this. We knew how to get things done; we were focused, resourceful, resilient, positive, kind, empathetic, respectful, honest and up front, and grateful. These attributes will take you far. Solid management skills always come in handy under any circumstance. Please remember these characteristics when dealing with your team daily. Coming from a good place will always reap rewards.

BEING AN ENLIGHTENED MANAGER IS NOT EASY. THERE CAN BE NEGATIVE CONSEQUENCES.

I once worked for an international financial firm. At the interview with the man who would become my boss, I told him that I was very proud of the fact that I had only let go one person in my entire management career. He just as proudly replied that he had fired numerous people throughout his stint, and that that was part of doing business. I knew then that this was not the ideal place for me, but I took the job anyhow because I needed it. In hindsight, I should have passed on this offer simply because of the cavalier attitude this new boss of mine had about letting employees go.

From day one, I was respectful and transparent with the team members, some of which had been working for this director and his managers for years on end. I immediately implemented new processes that were more efficient—with feedback from my colleagues and staff, of course. The first six months were fine, and it seemed as if my boss was okay with allowing me to do things my way. I later found out that he was extremely passive aggressive, and cunning. He had been in this role for twenty years, and he was determined to hang onto to it as long as possible, not letting anybody jeopardize his standing.

He was not confrontational or aggressive, always wearing a smile on his face, but he had no problem getting rid of those he felt were a threat to his authority. His superiors allowed him free reign to do as he pleased. He was the ultimate gatekeeper.

I had been told how abusive his trusted managers were toward the employees, and I soon saw this firsthand. They constantly harangued them, texted them at all hours of the night and day without compensation, and gossiped about them all behind their backs. It was a very disrespectful and dysfunctional operation.

I wanted to change things by example. I got input from all the staff about upcoming projects and long-standing duties and used their ideas. I let them make their own daily work decisions without micromanaging them. Many of these longtime team members thanked me for bringing in a new, positive, adult, respectful perspective to this workplace. I was proud of these accolades given to me.

Little did I know that behind the scenes, my boss, his go-to manager, and another supervisor were not happy about my management philosophy. They thought I was too lenient and that the team members were showing too much independence. My boss never came straight out and told me that this was the case, but when push came to shove, he let me go the first chance he had.

The team I oversaw was very saddened once they heard about my separation, and one of them even told me that I was the best manager she had ever had.

This management group I worked with those couple of years never trusted their staff, were top-down micromanagers, and always had ulterior power motives. An Enlightened Manager builds trust and loyalty, provides a place of dignity and respect, and always does the right thing no matter what the consequences may be.

My righthand person at that job kept in touch with me. She expressed to me how upset she was at how I had been treated. I assured her that I was going to be okay, which I was. She also told me that this incident made her re-evaluate her future aspirations. Did she want to continue working for these people?

Six months after I was laid off from the firm, she notified me that she had gotten a new job and was leaving that department and that she was glad to finally get away from that unenlightened director. She thanked me for inspiring her to make that change. I was very happy to have had this positive impact on her; this is the legacy of an Enlightened Manager.

Doing the right thing sounds simple enough, but in the work world, this may be looked at as weakness. Corporate America can be dog-eat-dog, and unfortunately, no one fully trusts one another in this highly competitive environment. We can change this, one Enlightened Manager at a time. All you have to do is promise never to waver from always treating people with complete respect and dignity.

CHAPTER 5: DISHONORABLE / NO-HOLDS-BARRED MANAGEMENT

NEGATIVE TRAITS IN AN ORGANIZATION THAT MUST BE ELIMINATED IMMEDIATELY:

- Disrespect
- Mistrust
- Gossip
- Meddling
- Instability
- Undermining
- Lies
- Inequality

RUNNING AMOK

I was once working for an organization that had hired this new "wunderkind" to revolutionize the department. Right off the bat, this person started laying people off and outsourcing vital jobs. The wunderkind had carte blanche, and there was no one there to rein in this person. In a very short time, wunderkind let go of some very talented, loyal, and downright good folks. The remaining staff were, of course, afraid of losing their jobs, too, so they sought and found positions elsewhere. This was an able and upwardly mobile group that could find other work quite easily.

Soon this department was understaffed and overwhelmed. The remaining managers were scrambling, trying to find training material on how to "retain staff." It was astonishing! How to retain staff? How about not building a mistrustful and insecure work environment in the first place?

They even reached out to some of the laid off workers to ask them to return to their old jobs. This wunderkind really had no idea how to manage but nonetheless was placed in this important position—a highly compensated executive who didn't even know basic or decent Management 101.

This scenario happens much too often in our corporate world, and it needs to stop. How someone new to an organization is allowed to just walk in and create utter chaos is absurd. No manager should ever have carte blanche to do whatever they wish, however pleasing it might sound on paper.

UNFETTERED AUTHORITY

A vindictive manager I came across rewarded those the manager liked and punished those this person didn't care for. One decent employee was denied a raise and bonus for two straight years simply because she was on this person's "bad side." Even though this staff member didn't deserve this treatment, the organization's executives never questioned these negative evaluations. This director abused this position of authority and got away with it repeatedly. The staff member spoke to HR and to her boss's boss about this mistreatment but was ignored at every turn.

After a while, this solid employee had enough and left the department. The rest of this team deplored working for this administrator but were all too afraid to speak up. The turnover rate in this department was very high, and there were numerous other HR complaints. How does this happen? Obviously, there was no oversight over this out-of-control manager.

This type of behavior from upper management happens much too often. Administrators must also be held accountable for behaving unethically toward their employees. We must manage managers much more closely to prevent abuses like this. We must stop assuming that upper management is always right. Abuse of power is a disease that needs to be eradicated at every instance.

The old-fashioned authoritarian "I'm the boss" mentality must finally be laid to rest.

This way of managing doesn't take intellect, creativity, or brains. Again, the number one reason people up and leave their job is because of bad bosses.

A very close friend of mine was shocked when she personally witnessed a brand-new director come into a department and right off the bat start mistreating solid, long-time employees and get away with it. This person was very well compensated and had an impressive résumé but turned out to be the worst possible person to lead this department.

The director immediately began micromanaging highly skilled staff; the team even started getting text messages about returning to their desks from their new boss while on bathroom breaks. This person would not accommodate personnel who were going through serious health issues, denying them alternative schedules to tend to their medical appointments. Mean-spiritedness at its absolute worst.

This boss brought on a person whom the director had personally known before, but in a matter of months, this new staff member went on stress leave themselves after being harangued by this former "friend." This new boss was intimidated by the dedicated and well-liked assistant director (AD) and acted quickly to sideline the AD by stripping away their authority, followed by an official demotion. Many unenlightened managers are deeply insecure and lash out to cover it up.

Almost immediately, there were numerous complaints against this new director. However, the executives who hired the director would not admit that they had made a mistake and allowed this person to continue with this horrendous behavior. The collateral damage was enormous: costly stress leaves, high turnover rate, low morale, lawsuits, chaos, and even this organization's credentialing stipulations were now at risk. After a while, it got so bad that the executives had to finally admit that there was a problem. Consultants were hired to evaluate the situation and then a very expensive "coach" was brought on to teach this director "how to manage." All of this was costing this organization dearly. The administrators sacrificed their entire staff for this one person whose only contribution was causing complete and utter havoc. It was sad and shocking.

As is the case in many of these scenarios, this organization's loss was another one's gain. The long-time assistant director who was very well liked and dedicated to the organization, and whom this horrible director had demoted, had had enough and found a director position at a different organization. The entire staff was heartbroken, as the only person in a position of authority in that department who knew what they were doing was now leaving.

This institution's executives were irresponsibly arrogant. They refused to own up to their mistake of hiring this bad manager in the first place and then allowed this person to practically destroy the department in a few months, a department that took many years of hard work to build. It may seem unbelievable, but this actually happened.

Twenty percent of workers say they face hostile or threatening environments at work.
—2015 American Working Conditions Survey

It's mindboggling how some organizations put up with abuses of power by their management teams. The immense harm to staff, morale, and productivity costs these companies billions of dollars a year, and they can't even see it. They need to open their eyes. It's bad for business! It's bad for society!

> **Surgeon General Vivek Murthy says workplaces are taking a toll on American's mental and physical health.**
> **"A healthy workforce is the foundation for thriving organizations and healthier communities,"** **Murthy said, according to the Report on Workplace Well-Being.**

PLEASE, BE HUMAN!

I once worked for an independent tech advertising company, reporting directly to the proprietors. Before I came on board, the staff and owners had worked together for many years. From the outside, it looked like everything was good. But when push came to shove at crunch time, the owners showed their true colors.

A couple of months after I was hired, the company started losing business, and the proprietors panicked. This was during the 2009 economic downturn. The very first thing they did was furlough the entire staff; we were now only working and getting paid for thirty-two hours a week. This was an economic blow to all of us. The employees were willing to make this sacrifice to make sure that the company survived. But instead of rallying the troops, the owners began behaving like dictators; "take it or leave it" was their attitude. They figured that the economy was so bad that the staff had nowhere else to go. Wrong approach!

I'm certain that if they had been sincere, sat people down, and were honest about what was happening and what their plan was to get back to normal, the staff would have understood and done all they could to help. But instead, they started firing people in place of laying them off. They did this to save on unemployment claims. They were ecstatic when an elderly employee, who had worked for them for many years, was denied unemployment benefits because they fought the claim. Complete monsters.

Since they took the "my way or the highway" approach, many people, including myself, took the highway, finding new jobs and leaving this organization understaffed and not ready to handle the demand when the work returned.

I can't emphasize enough how respect, sincerity, empathy, and fairness can help weather any storm. Always treat your staff respectfully, under all circumstances. They will appreciate it and will give you that respect right back.

Seventy-two percent of employees surveyed rated respectful treatment of all employees at all levels as very important. This was the top contributor to overall employee satisfaction.
— Society for Human Resources Management
2014 survey

Respect is the number one behavior, above all others, that would lead to greater employee engagement and commitment.
—*Harvard Business Review*
(survey of 20,000 employees)

CHAPTER 6:
ENLIGHTENED MANAGERS IN ACTION

AN ENLIGHTENED MANAGER IN ACTION

One day, a good friend of mine told me that she was very stressed at her job of eleven years. Almost from the onset, she had had an assistant whom she relied on to help with her job duties. Recently, her assistant had gotten another job and the organization's leaders did not want to fill the open position; they wanted to save money by eliminating that job. My friend now had to work extra hours during the week and on weekends just to keep up.

It was obvious that the leaders of this company had no idea how my friend was going to be impacted by their callous decision. However, my friend's immediate boss was on her side; she agreed that the assistant position was vital to their department. She went to bat for my friend, fighting tooth and nail to get the job requisition approved. This went on for quite a while.

Even though my friend's manager kept her abreast of the progress of their quest, my friend was at her wit's end; if she didn't get a full-time assistant soon, she was seriously thinking of leaving that job. Her manager understood this and valued her as an employee. She kept fighting.

The manager helped by hiring temps and by filling in herself. My friend and her manager were a great team, contributing trust, respect, empathy, and transparency from both ends. My friend knew that her boss was doing everything in her power to make the situation right, so she hung in there.

After several months of going back and forth, my friend's manager finally succeeded in changing their leadership's mind. My friend was ecstatic. She told me that even though she was stressed, basically working two jobs to keep things running, what gave her hope at every turn was the unflinching support that her manager showed her through it all. This is an Enlightened Manager at work. She showed great compassion and empathy toward her direct report and persevered to make things right for her. How motivating it is—to know that your boss has your back.

Go to bat for your employees, even if it's not easy. It's the right thing to do. A manager's support, or lack thereof, makes a huge difference in an employee's outlook and productivity. Be there for them every step of the way. They deserve it.

Below is an example of an Enlightened Manager working her magic. Taken from a personal account from someone I interviewed.

From the moment I shared with my manager that I was pregnant, I received nothing but respect, compassion, shared happiness, and total support. Whenever I had doctor's appointments, which were weekly, my boss was understanding and would let me either come in later or leave earlier. I always felt comfortable asking her about my needs during my pregnancy; I didn't feel scared or that I was a bother.

She took the time to explain my health insurance and my leave benefits; made sure that I understood how much I would be paid during this period; helped me keep track of my vacation days so I would have enough time when I did go on leave; and emphasized that I needed to continue paying my insurance while still working, so I would not have to worry about it while away. She also knew I took the train to work and that I would normally get to work around 8 a.m., even though I start at 9 a.m. So, whenever I hadn't arrived at my usual time, she would text me to make sure I was okay.

My boss really cares about me; she shows this day in and day out. When my leave was up, I made the decision to come back part time, if I could. I wasn't sure that it would be okay since there was so much work. I was welcomed back with open arms and my request to work part time was granted. I feel extremely grateful and lucky to have such a wonderful manager, especially during this momentous time in my life when I needed the support the most.

Human interaction at its very best! An Enlightened Manager sincerely cares about their people and shows it daily.

MERCILESS MANAGING OFFSET BY MANAGING WITH GREAT EMPATHY

One's personal life and one's job are not always distinct; one is tied to the other, no matter what we've been taught. "It's not personal, it's just business" is not accurate whatsoever. What happens at work affects your private life and vice versa. When work is not going well, it will seep into your home life; if you lose your job, it will definitely affect your family's well-being. So, it's essential to understand that work and home life are intertwined. It's all personal.

Many years ago, my family was going through one of the most difficult moments in our lives. Our dear mother was terminally ill, and we were all doing our best to deal with this dire situation. On top of this, my eldest sister was having problems at her job. During this trying period, her immediate boss was harassing her at work. Yes, her performance was suffering; understandably, her job duties were not her top priority at the time. My sister's boss knew the situation but still didn't let up. She kept hounding her for every little thing: "Where is this report?" "You did this wrong. Do it again." "It's still not right." This manager rode my sister until she couldn't take it any longer and snapped.

On the morning that my sister returned to work after burying our mother, the unenlightened manager entered her office to continue the harassment, when suddenly my sister yelled at the top of her lungs. She told her manager, with many expletives, to get out of her office and leave her alone.

The manager was shocked. She immediately ran to the owner of the firm and demanded that he fire my sister on the spot. The owner refused the manager's request. He told her that my sister was a very solid, long-time employee whose mother had just passed away and that she needed some sympathy at this time. The manager remained adamant; she wanted my sister fired for insubordination and threatened to quit if her request was not satisfied.

The owner did not waver and accepted the bad manager's resignation on the spot. On top of losing our precious mother, my sister almost lost her livelihood. This would have made her life immensely worse. I will forever be grateful to this Enlightened Proprietor who showed empathy and humanity when needed most. He truly left a lasting impact on my sister's life.

Please always show empathy toward your staff. Before anything else, we are all human beings, so we must treat one another as such, even and especially at work.

WHEN IT'S ALL SAID AND DONE...

I once managed a woman who was approaching the end of her career. She was very knowledgeable but could at times be a bit brusque when interacting with some of the other staff. She had been around a long time and was planning on retiring in a couple of years, so she didn't put up with any nonsense. I respected her tremendously; she had paid her dues, and I was going to make sure that her time left with us was going to be as positive as possible. We developed a wonderful working relationship; we had a true partnership. Unfortunately, before she got to retire, she was diagnosed with cancer.

I got a chance to visit her at the hospital. We talked about work and life in general; she had an amazing story, and I enjoyed every second with her that evening. To be able to spend time with her at that moment of her life was a humbling experience.

Before I left, we hugged, and she thanked me for being a good boss to her. We knew that we'd probably never see each other again, so tears streamed down both our faces. It is something I will never forget.

Walking back to my car that evening, I felt sad but also happy that I had made someone's life a little bit better, Monday through Friday, nine to five. This is what it's always been about for me: treating people with the utmost respect and dignity at every single point of my existence. I will never waver from this.

A few days later, her son notified us that she had passed away. We were devastated by the news.

Every day of our lives, no matter where, we have the choice to treat people decently. It is something that will be part of your final story, good or bad. How will you be remembered?

> **"Don't aspire to make a living,
> aspire to make a difference."**
> —Denzel Washington

ACKNOWLEDGMENTS

I want to thank my wonderful wife, Omolola, for inspiring me every day to continue in the pursuit of my lifelong dreams and aspirations. My supportive family—Mrs. O, Ninfa, Liz, Pat, Cesar, Giuliana, Dayo, Lissette, Michael, Isabella, Alessandra, and Mateo. They mean the world to me. My dearest friends Adriana and Sharrieff for their ongoing support. To amazing colleagues whom I connected with throughout the years, Dahmenah, Marisha, Ara, Eddie, Nancy, Ivy, Elisa, Laura, Vilma, Diana, Reggie, Karen, Greg, Paul, Dana, Joseph, Jeff, Maria G., and Esther. To those who contributed to the making of this book. Kris Avilla for her beautiful cover design, Jessica Lott for sharing her successful management insights, and Nicole Frail for her masterful copy editing. And to all the wonderful people who I crossed paths within my work life, you made it good.

ABOUT THE AUTHOR

Alejandro Diaz was born and raised in working-class Chicago to Mexican immigrant parents. He holds an MFA in screenwriting from the University of Miami and a bachelor of arts from the University of Illinois at Chicago (UIC). He lives in California with his wife.

Alejandro is a seasoned manager who has more than thirty-five years of experience in a variety of industries working with multinationals, marketing firms, nonprofits, healthcare organizations, including companies such as UPS, Kaiser Permanente, Gannett, and KPMG. He's worked closely with RNs, MBAs, project managers, sales teams, dock workers, union employees, social workers, physicians, IT personnel, programmers, independent proprietors, managers, directors, and vice presidents. Alejandro's expertise has saved organizations time and money while also creating an atmosphere of good faith, trust, and efficiency among the staff. Through his personal and professional experiences, he brings a unique perspective to the workplace. With tenacity, drive, and optimism, his goal is to take a company to a place of respect, dignity, and effectiveness, with camaraderie, and of course, success. Many of his insights may seem like common sense, but it actually takes time and hard work to transform a dysfunctional culture into one that is open, honest, respectful, and productive. There is an art to becoming an Enlightened Manager. With the right vision, anyone can learn this art and utilize it. His hope is that this book will give you the tools to create an honorable and fruitful work environment for all.

Alejandro is available for speaking engagements, conducting workshops, coaching, mentoring, and training managers. Please visit his website to learn more about his mission of Embracing Humanity in the Workplace. https://dandems.com